CLINGMANS DOME

HIGHEST MOUNTAIN
IN THE GREAT SMOKIES

MARCI SPENCER
FOREWORD BY GEORGE ELLISON

natural
HISTORY PRESS

Honorable Thomas Lanier Clingman (July 27, 1812–November 3, 1897). *Library of Congress.*

To the Southwest of the gorges through which the Big Pigeon [River] escapes from the mountains, the chain rises rapidly in high pointed peaks and sharp ridges...This is the beginning of the Smoky Mt. Chain proper, which by general elevation of both its peaks and its crest, by its perfect continuity, its great roughness and difficulty of approach, may be called the master chain of the Appalachian System. For over 50 miles it forms a high and almost impervious barrier between Tennessee and North Carolina...only one tolerable road reaches its summit, Road Gap...Beyond Road Gap, the chain of the Smoky Mts. Rises still higher...About six miles South-west of the Gap is the culminating point of the Smoky Mts.: Smoky Dome or Clingmans Mt...

Professor Arnold Guyot, "Notes on the Geography of the Mountain District of Western North Carolina," February 22, 1863 (published in *North Carolina Historical Review* 15, July 1938, submitted by Myron Avery and Kenneth S. Boardman).

Published by Natural History
A Division of The History Press
Charleston, SC 29403
www.historypress.net

Copyright © 2013 by Marci Spencer
Foreword copyright © 2013 by George Ellison
All rights reserved

Front cover: Courtesy of Bill Vinson, Red Chair Architects.
Back cover: Photo by Bill Lea. Inset: GSMNP archives.

First published 2013

ISBN 978.1.5402.2128.5

Library of Congress CIP data applied for.

Notice: The information in this book is true and complete to the best of our knowledge. It is offered without guarantee on the part of the author or The History Press. The author and The History Press disclaim all liability in connection with the use of this book.

All rights reserved. No part of this book may be reproduced or transmitted in any form whatsoever without prior written permission from the publisher except in the case of brief quotations embodied in critical articles and reviews.

CONTENTS

Foreword. "Elbow Room for the Soul," by George Ellison — 7
Acknowledgements — 13
Introduction — 17

1. Measuring a Mountain — 21
2. Removing a Forest — 35
3. Building a Tower — 51
4. Exploring an Ecosystem — 69
5. Hosting an Uninvited Guest — 85
6. Finding a Flower or Two — 95
7. Denning on the Dome: A Bear's Tale — 111
8. Building a Mountain — 121
9. Monitoring Air and Water — 129
10. Following a Trail — 137
11. Enjoying the View — 155

Appendix. Checklist of Plants and Animals Referenced in Text — 167
Bibliography — 171
Index — 185
About the Author — 191

FOREWORD
"ELBOW ROOM FOR THE SOUL"

Ap-pa-la-chi-an...
no one really knows what it
means...but all will agree
it is a beautiful name for an
elegant mountain chain.

All of the six-thousand-foot peaks in eastern North America—excepting Mount Washington in New Hampshire—are located in Western North Carolina or east Tennessee or both. It is a land of high vistas—vantage points that enable us to rise above everyday experience, take in some grand scenery, maybe see a hawk or two and study the lay of the land. As was once observed, "There's wonder and delight up there...elbow room for the soul."

Where are we? A full appreciation of the southern mountains—especially the Great Smokies and Clingmans Dome—can't be had without some understanding of their place in the interrelated landscape of mountain ranges and peaks and valleys we call the Appalachians.

Broad-winged hawks bound for Bolivia and Peru follow south-by-southwestward routes each fall, riding updrafts and tailwinds over all, or portions, of the nearly 1,500-mile extent of the Appalachians, from the Gaspe Peninsula in Canada to its terminus in Alabama south of Birmingham. From Canada to just south of the state line between New York and Pennsylvania, they pass over the shining lakes and scoured rocky terrain of the once glaciated Northern Appalachians. They soon arrive (a few miles

Foreword

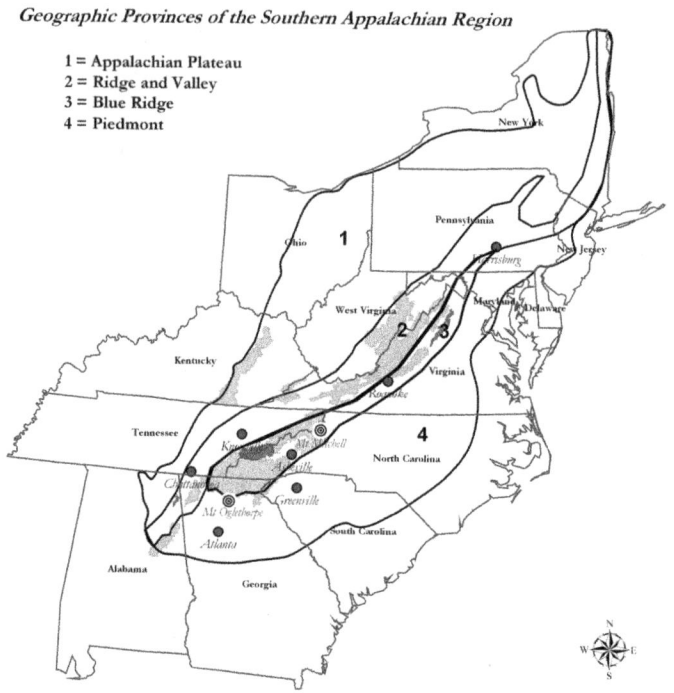

Geographic Provinces of the Southern Appalachian Region

1 = Appalachian Plateau
2 = Ridge and Valley
3 = Blue Ridge
4 = Piedmont

north of Harrisburg, Pennsylvania) at the approximate demarcation line between the Northern Appalachians and the four geographic provinces of the Southern Appalachians.

Appalachian landscapes south of north-central Pennsylvania at Hickory Run State Park were never truly glaciated. But eighteen thousand years ago, during the Wisconsin stage of the last ice age—with mean annual temperatures below thirty-two degrees Fahrenheit—it was cold enough in the Smokies and adjacent ranges to have a tree line at five thousand feet and permafrost with tundra vegetation above that elevation.

At this juncture, the broad-wings have decisions to make. Some few veer off course to the southeast and travel over the worn foothills of the Piedmont province—the eroded eastern rim of the nearly 275-million-year-old Appalachians—from southeastern Maryland to Georgia. Most follow the natural corridors of the Ridge and Valley province down the Shenandoah and Tennessee Valleys or take a shortcut over the low-lying Cumberland Plateau, that portion of the Plateau province south of the Cumberland Gap.

Others continue due south along the spine of the Southern Appalachians into the Blue Ridge province, which extends six hundred miles from Harrisburg, Pennsylvania, to Mount Oglethorpe in Georgia, thirty miles north of Atlanta. Geographers subdivide the Blue Ridge into Northern (NBR) and Southern (SBR) provinces. Less than five miles wide in places, the NBR extends from Harrisburg through Maryland to the Roanoke River Gap, where the SBR suddenly expands into a vast and complex sea of ranges, peaks, cross-ridges, escarpments, gorges, valleys and coves two hundred miles in length and up to seventy-five miles in width.

Gaining altitude in a thermal, the hawks circle over the very heart of one of the most diverse temperate zones (in regard to flora and distinctive natural areas) on this planet. Near where the steep eastern flank of the Blue Ridge escarpment descends into the western Piedmont, Mount Mitchell at 6,684 feet looms in the Black Mountains, while out to the west the outline of Clingmans Dome at 6,643 feet hovers on the state line between North Carolina and Tennessee. To the north of the Smokies along the line are the Iron and Bald ranges. To the south along the line are the Unicois and Unakas and down in Georgia, the Cohuttas. Much of the entire front from the Iron to the Cohuttas is wild and remote, the sort of setting that out west they call "big country." But the Smokies, seventy miles long and as much as twenty-five or so miles wide, with peak after peak rising above five thousand feet and encompassing upward of 575,000 acres (not excluding the 50,000 or so acres of low-lying foothills never incorporated into the national park), are what old-time surveyors called the "Master Range"—that is, the most massive mountain range in eastern North America, the keystone of the Southern Appalachians.

So, "where are we" again? Let's go through it one more time. Here we are on Clingmans Dome at 6,643 feet, the third-highest peak in the East, astride a massive range called the Smokies, within the Great Smoky Mountains National Park, on the western front of the Southern Blue Ridge province—one of the four geographic provinces in the unglaciated Southern Appalachians that co-joins in Pennsylvania with the glaciated Northern Appalachians to compose the 1,500-mile-long mountain chain we know as the Appalachians. With this book in hand, Clingmans Dome becomes the ideal vantage point from which to observe and better understand this ancient and elegant terrain.

As a high vista, the tower at Clingmans Dome is perhaps equaled elsewhere but never in my experience surpassed. Ask someone to describe what he or

Foreword

she most clearly remembers after visiting Clingmans Dome, and they will almost invariably say, "The view from the tower." Ask what they remember seeing, and the reply will be something like, "The Smokies" or "Beautiful mountains." They would be hard-pressed if asked to be more specific.

That will change with the publication of this book. The closing chapter, titled "Enjoying the View," is given over to annotated descriptions (with schematic maps) of historic sites, towns, rivers, lakes, mountain peaks and ranges as viewed from north, east, south and west. On a bright sunshiny day from the tower atop the third-highest peak in eastern North America, you can see Mount Mitchell, the highest at 6,684 feet, seventy-three miles to the east. Clingmans Dome used to be in second place but was not long ago nosed out by Mount Craig (adjacent to Mount Mitchell), 6,647 feet, in a topological squabble over the never-ending geomorphic issue concerning the question, "When does a ridge become a mountain?"—or vice versa.

My favorite direction to contemplate from the tower is the "Southern View." There's Andrews Bald (figure "A" on the schematic map), one and a half miles away on Forney Ridge in the national park. There's Fontana Lake (figure "E"), just eight or so miles away. You can't see Bryson City, but you can see Fry Mountain (figure "B"), which the town backs up to fourteen miles away. Did I mention my house? If you look ten or so miles to the southeast, you can almost see it tucked in behind a ridge where a creek with its headwaters on the southeastern flank of Clingmans flows out of the national park past my front door and into the Tuckasegee River in winter or Fontana Lake in summer on its way to the Gulf of Mexico. We have lived in the virtual shadow of Clingmans for thirty-seven years and counting. So the materialization, as it were, of this book at this time is of particular interest.

Marci Spencer drove over from her home at Old Fort, east of Asheville, last year to visit at my office in Bryson City and discuss her ideas for a book.

I asked, "Why Clingmans Dome?...It's one hundred miles from where you live." She explained that she was a volunteer worker for the Great Smoky Mountains National Park assigned to Clingmans Dome. Even I can do the math on that. She was driving two hundred miles round-trip to work as a park volunteer. It was clear she had become infatuated with the place—enough so that she wanted to write a book about Clingmans Dome. People sometimes tell me about books they want to write. I enjoy talking and offering encouragement. But all too soon stuff happens—spirits dampen, and it's not as easy as it looks. I remember, however, telling my wife, "This might happen...from what I've seen of it, she can write. She's obviously determined…and she's doing it for all the right reasons," or something like that. And here we are now with a fine book about Clingmans Dome, written and entering the final editorial stages before publication. I can't remember whether she asked me to write a foreword or if I offered to do so if a book was ever in hand. Doesn't matter. Here I sit not far from Clingmans Dome more than pleased to be writing one. And I don't have a lot more to say before I'll get out of the way and let the book speak for itself.

Our mountains and mountain ranges here in the Southern Blue Ridge—the ones we see every day or visit at every opportunity—are like prominent musicians, literary luminaries or public figures of any sort whom we admire.

We want to know more about them, what makes them tick, how they got to be how they are and what their futures hold in store. So we read their biographies (their life stories): Maurice Brooks or Scott Weidensaul on the Appalachians; Charlton Ogburn on the Southern Appalachians; Michael Frome, Margaret Brown, Dan Pierce or Rose Houk on the Smokies; Ken Wise and Ron Peterson (jointly) on Mount Le Conte; Bob Zahner on Whiteside Mountain; Jennifer Laughin on Roan Mountain; Miles Tager on Grandfather Mountain; and S. Kent Schwarzkoph and Timothy Silver on Mount Mitchell and the Black Mountains. And now we have Marci Spencer on Clingmans Dome.

From here on, in order to avoid confusion between the book title and the mountain, I'll use *Kuwahi* or "Mulberry Place"—the designation almost always used in source guides for place names in Cherokee lore. It is also a way of honoring their ongoing relationship with the spirit of a mountain that traditionalist Freeman Owle (in his story "The Magic Lake") prefers to call *Skahonige* or "Blue Mountain"—a pretty name perhaps all the more appropriate in that red mulberry trees never grow above three thousand feet, if that, in the Smokies. By any name, however, it was a sacred retreat. The great white bear that walked (and sometimes talked) like a man lived there. Outspread below was a mist-shrouded enchanted lake in which wounded bears were restored to health. It was also a *hibernaculum*, a place of winter refuge where the bears danced in late autumn before retiring into the mountain to sleep and dream until spring came again.

Marci Spencer's *Clingmans Dome: The Highest Mountain in the Great Smokies* is every bit as thorough, informative and entertaining as it ought to be—exactly the sort of book that *Kuwahi* and the bears deserve—worthy of joining those by the authors mentioned here. (See citations for each in the bibliography.) Writing the "biography" of a place so widely known and written about in popular and scientific publications could not have been an easy task. Her energy and appetite for researching and processing a wide range of sources is obvious. The next step of organizing the information into a coherent story was handled in a dutiful manner. Historical topics and events are, for the most part, arranged chronologically. General topics pertaining to wildlife, flora, ecosystems and environmental issues were inserted where they seemed to fit. I'm confident she was ably assisted in these matters by the editorial staff at The History Press, from whose advice I have also benefited from time to time.

The main storyline, of course, follows events atop Clingmans Dome, especially the history of the tower itself and environmental concerns such as the near demise of the Fraser fir. But along the way, there will be almost everything and anyone you can imagine. One of my favorite flowers appears in the sixth chapter, "Finding a Flower…or Two." The flower that needed to be found was Rugel's Indian plantain (*Rugelia nudicaulis*), "which grows in GSMNP and nowhere else on the planet," Spencer advises. But in places along high elevation ridges, it proves to be locally abundant. The flower nods from the top of a one-foot stem. It is, she admits, "dull yellow…with long straggly brown stigmas." Unwilling to categorize Rugel's Indian plantain as a drab or maybe even ugly flower (which it is), she diverts attention to the "embroidered" ground-hugging leaves and advises the reader to remember that "the beauty nature deprived in bud, she compensated in leaves…Let no one claim Rugel's is unattractive."

Because of the lively manner in which the book is written, the inherent level of interest in this sort of subject matter and the wide range of source materials having to do with the human and natural history—not just of *Kuwahi* but of the region as a whole—it's a given that Marci Spencer's work will be widely read and used as a resource for many years.

George Ellison
Bryson City, North Carolina
February 11, 2013

ACKNOWLEDGEMENTS

One cannot write the history of a mountain like Clingmans Dome and the Great Smoky Mountains National Park without the help from many who know it well. Stacks of books, journals and research reports; Internet resources; libraries; museums; and filled notebook-after-notebook are just not enough. Clingmans' history is too rich, too precious and too dynamic to write the story alone. Those educated souls who have dedicated their life's work to protecting and preserving the park and its treasures know best.

Chapters on the spruce-fir forest ecosystem, high-elevation flora, air and water quality, bears and balsam woolly adelgids could not have been written without the advice, guidance, support and review of National Park Service (NPS) biologists, botanists and specialists, such as Kristine Johnson, Glenn Taylor, Paul Super, Susan Sachs, Janet Rock, Bill Stiver, Joe Yarkovich, Jim Renfro and Matt Kulp. Tom Robbins, retired NPS ranger, still remembered for his guided history walks at Clingmans Dome, provided his insight and critique of the chapters on logging, explorations and tower construction.

The NPS is fortunate to have such a knowledgeable, dedicated steward in Annette Hartigan, in care of its priceless historical documents. Her diligent attention, encouragement and assistance at the Great Smoky Mountains National Park Library/Archives fed my curiosity and inspired my historical research.

Much appreciation goes to geologists Scott Southworth, Harry L. Moore and James Wedekind for sharing their expertise and reviewing the relevant chapter. Each has studied the geology of the Great Smoky Mountains and was patient with my rudimental climb up my geological learning curve.

Acknowledgements

Logging chapter salutes go to Jim Thurston of the Little River Railroad and Lumber Co. Museum for my logging education and for his time-consuming photographic help. Jerry Ledford provided an in-depth, personal, little-known look into Norwood Lumber Co.'s logging on Forney Creek. Ron Sullivan put down his own pen and interrupted his own writing pursuits on the GSM logging/railroad history to immediately answer every e-mail question I posed—like a time-honored friend.

Many thanks are due to my son, Tim Worsham, for the numerous communications and meticulous attention to his detailed pen-and-ink illustrations. Thanks to Dad for opening my eyes, not just to the mountains and the majestic oak but also to the rocks and roots that define that mountain, and the marks on the bark and the leaf on the twigs that give character to that oak.

To my daughter, Christi Worsham, and granddaughter, Brooke Lyda, I thank you dearly for hiking all the trails discussed in this book, sometimes more than once—especially Mother's Day 2012, in a heavy, forty-eight-degree downpour on the Appalachian Trail (A.T.) from Clingmans Dome to Newfound Gap. Thanks for smiling when two-day hikes were squeezed into one and thirty-minute delays became sixty whenever I found a new flower, bird or tree.

I am grateful to my husband, John Spencer, for picking me up when I stumbled, listening to every edit of every chapter, keeping me focused, saying "yes" when the thoughts were "no" and shouldering weight when tasks were tough. Thank you for following me to museums, libraries, newspaper offices, interviews and more—and for "living on the Dome" at the farm for the past few years.

Thanks to those who've added their "voices" to the text: Ila Hatter, well-known GSM naturalist/herbalist who teaches native plant cooking; Jerry Ledford, a descendant of the lumber company that logged Clingmans' south face; Jared Laufenberg, biologist with UT Bear Research Program; and Danny Bernstein, retired professor, now long-distance hiker and author.

Scott Dean, field botanist and educator with North Carolina Arboretum's Blue Ridge Naturalist's Program, encouraged me to not just identify a plant but also come to know it. Ken Wise and Dr. Ron Peterson at University of Tennesee–Knoxville sent me in the right direction numerous times in my quest for accurate information. So did Steve Kemp with Great Smoky Mountains Association, Glenn Cardwell, Dr. Dan Pitillo, Jeff Wadley and the Smoky Mountain Historical Society.

Appalachian State University mycologist Dr. Coleman McCleneghan, North Carolina Wildlife Resource Commission wildlife biologist Chris Kelly,

Acknowledgements

Sue Cameron at U.S. Fish and Wildlife Services and North American Bear Center biologist Sue Mansfield are all gratefully acknowledged for their respective help and review of truffles, flying squirrels, moss spiders and black bears. Thanks to Brian Terrell at TDOT for creating the stateline map. Hundreds of nameless e-mail and phone contacts are not forgotten.

My heartfelt appreciation is extended to the friends and family of Hubert Bebb, the architect of Clingmans Dome Tower—Heather Burkhart, great-granddaughter; Ellen Bebb, niece; Lee Mellor of Buckhorn Inn; Tom Trotter of Trotter and Associates, Architect; and Bob Vinson of Community Tectonics (now Red Chair Architects)—for their time and support in helping me pay tribute to a fine gentleman.

Dr. Thomas Jeffrey, associate director and senior editor for Thomas A. Edison Papers at Rutgers University, New Jersey, receives a special note of gratitude. Finding someone alive who "knew" Thomas Clingman well was challenging. In his research for his book on Clingman and several articles for the *North Carolina Historical Review*, Dr. Jeffrey became quite acquainted with Senator Clingman. Thanks for your help with my chapter on Thomas Lanier Clingman, giving proper respect, credit and voice to the man whose name is recognized as the highest mountain in the Great Smoky Mountains.

As a NPS volunteer "stationed" at Clingmans Dome, I'd like to speak for all Dome volunteers to extend our gratitude to our supervisors, Florie Takaki and Lynda Doucette, and our volunteer coordinators, Dana Soehn (former) and Christine Hoyer (present), for their patience with us and their dedicated service to GSMNP.

I extend my utmost appreciation to J. Banks Smither at The History Press for his unfailing support, guidance and encouragement throughout the publication process. Others at The History Press, too, helped make *Clingmans Dome* a reality. Thank you, Darcy Mahan, as my copyeditor, for your attentive scrutiny of the text and constructive improvements.

Early in the research process, George Ellison invited me to his office in Bryson City, North Carolina. Slipping around and through stacks of resource materials about the Smokies that he'd put aside for the visit, I made it across the room. Across the desk, mounded high with more books, we quickly recognized a shared love for the Smokies.

"Clingmans Dome has always been a special place to me," he said. "I lead wildflower walks up there, you know." More books were pulled from tightly packed shelves as we talked. From *North with the Spring*, by Edwin Way Teale, George Ellison read:

Acknowledgements

Fifty miles northwest of the ridges where the warblers fed and nested, the Great Smokies straddle the North Carolina–Tennessee line. Sixteen of their peaks rise above 6,000 feet. Five overtop famed Mt. Washington. To climb the highest of these, Clingmans Dome, in the spring is equivalent to moving backwards more than a month or jumping northward more than half a thousand miles in space...As we left the car and climbed the path...the fog and the woods were filled with a sound like a musical creaking axle, a long unwinding birdsong, sweet and tumbling forth, a song that went on and on as though it would never end. All though the upper Smokies we heard this song repeated without once seeing the singer...

George Ellison looked up. Neither spoke; we just smiled. Both of us recognized a mutual friend.

When a reviewer completed my manuscript, she remarked, "You can certainly tell that you love this mountain."

I do.

INTRODUCTION

It was more than luck. It was "Potluck." Sleek, tapered wings designed for speed propelled him through heavy Smoky Mountain rain. Strong natural instincts told him where to go. "Potluck" was going home. When World War I telegraphs failed or were unavailable, homing pigeons flew through snow, hail or bullets to deliver war messages from camp to base. Like military carrier pigeons, "Potluck" was on assignment. Tied to his leg in a tiny, aluminum capsule was an important message. Set aloft from Clingmans Dome at 1:20 p.m. on Sunday, June 9, 1929, "Potluck" banked into his final approach, landing on his loft platform in Asheville, North Carolina, at 4:28 p.m. With soaking wet feathers and drooping wings, he rested in the hands of J.R. Horne as the canister was removed. The message delivered read:

> *1929, June 9. Clingmans Dome 1 p.m.:* arrived Dome exactly same time as Knoxville party. Built fire, lunched, exchanged letters per schedule. Erected Kephart Memorial on big spruce tree on trail on state line. Struck heavy rain 2 hours after leaving Conner's place Saturday. Rain continued for most of the afternoon and night. Pitched camp in rain. Everything and everybody got soaked. Big fire helped some. Fairly good night considering miserable conditions. All party well and feeling good today, but mostly heavy fog and mist with little rain. Turning back to Indian Gap this afternoon instead of pushing on to Silers Bald. Must put base camp in good condition and dry out before making any more side trips. Have already had several

Introduction

interesting experiences but we can't seem to get much done in this rainy weather. Dense fog over Clingmans Dome. Pigeons got soaked with rest of us, but their appetite is good. So, guess they're all right.

Cheerio—W.S.A.

June 9, 1929, recorded the beginning of the Smokies' "Goodwill and Exploration Tour." Atop Clingmans Dome, staff from the *Knoxville News-Sentinel* greeted employees from the *Asheville Times*. A crudely built, wooden surveyor's tower capped the summit. Over a bronze plaque placed by surveyors to identify the Dome's highest point, letters from each governor were exchanged. Tennessee governor Harry H. Horton wrote, "Nothing is closer to the heart of Tennessee than the consummation and preservation of this great National Park in all its unrivaled beauty… [to] the honor of both states and …the nation and an inspiration for…generations."

North Carolina governor O. Max Gardner agreed, writing, "How intriguing it is that the greetings of the governors of Tennessee and North Carolina should be exchanged on the state line in the heart of the Great Smoky Mountains National Park area, in a marvelous primeval wilderness and on the Dome of one of the highest peaks in eastern America!…North Carolina and Tennessee have this great mountain treasure in common. The Great Smoky Mountains National Park movement was successful because of the visions and the public-spirited enterprises on the part of the citizens of our two states."

Symbolic handshakes across the state lines vowed mutual goals. The Tennessee–North Carolina state line had sliced Clingmans Dome in half. Now, by jointly pledging a commitment to a new national park, the Dome was cemented back together to rise as the highest mountain in Great Smoky Mountains National Park (GSMNP).

The *Knoxville News-Sentinel* crew returned to Gatlinburg, hiking twenty-four soggy miles in one day. *Asheville Times* sponsored its party on a twenty-five-day, 175-mile exploratory expedition, carrying a wicker basket with seven more homing pigeons to relay their discoveries back home.

Promises had been made on Clingmans Dome that day. Preserve a northern boreal forest living on high Smoky summits since the last great glacial period. Preserve the great biodiversity of life that lives in the coves, valleys and slopes below those summits.

Honor a culture. Respect a mountaintop revered by the Cherokee. Clingmans Dome, or "Kawahi," Cherokee believed, was the gathering place of black bears before hibernating for the winter. Below Clingmans Dome was a sacred lake with healing powers.

Introduction

This is the story of a mountain preserved in the heart of the Great Smoky Mountains. Low clouds hang like halos, fog-filled valleys mound up like whipped cream and misty days outnumber clear ones. Westerly winds gust over rugged slopes. Blue ridge upon blue ridge soften the mood and ease the mind. Steep trails test perseverance and resolve. And mountains, both near and distant, offer their own invitations.

High altitudes create blustery, frigid winters, with strong, damaging winds. Growing seasons are short, and forest floor sunlight is minimal. To live here, plants and animals either require such harsh elements for survival or have adapted to withstand them.

But despite these extremes, many have come: Thomas Clingman, Arnold Guyot, settlers, loggers, the railroad, Franklin Delano Roosevelt, the Civilian Conservation Corps, surveyors, architects, explorers, scientists, naturalists, rangers, superintendents, hikers, families and a national park.

Clingmans Dome Visitor Center. *Illustration by Tim Worsham.*

Introduction

This is the story of a mountain—explored by the curious, measured by the ambitious, towered by the creative, climbed by the hardiest, catalogued by the scientists, exploited by the greedy, ravaged by unwanted pests and loved by Cherokee Indians forced west, clinging to ancestral roots.

Why have you come? Turn the page. Discover Clingmans Dome.

CHAPTER 1

MEASURING A MOUNTAIN

Dark firs, much larger than their Canadian relatives, covered the domed summit, rising 150 feet and shadowing the forest floor. No road or trail led to the top of this massive mountain guarded by thick undergrowth. Only an occasional bear path parted tangled vegetation.

In 1858, Smoky Dome crowned the Southern Appalachian Range, reigning over one of the most rugged wilderness areas in the east. That year, Thomas Lanier Clingman and his companions came to the Great Smoky Mountains to measure the height of Smoky Dome. Professor Arnold Guyot, an experienced geographer from Princeton College, had been invited, but Guyot was measuring other mountains that year and couldn't join them.

Thomas Clingman's professional and personal experiences had prepared him for this excursion. Born in 1812 in Huntsville, North Carolina, Clingman was provided the best education that money could offer at a time when access to education was limited. With a sharp mind and an eagerness to learn, he advanced quickly. Excelling in chemistry, mathematics, public speaking, natural sciences and legal studies at the University of North Carolina at Chapel Hill, Clingman graduated at the top of his class in June 1832.

Dissatisfied with a small law practice in his hometown, Clingman craved more public exposure. In 1836, he moved to Asheville. Asheville, he decided, would be home for the rest of his life. A law practice in Asheville, however, did not satisfy his ambitions. Articulate, bright, principled and self-possessed, he sought power and success in politics. Election to the United States Senate was his first interest. But his ultimate goal was to become president of the United States.

For twenty years, Clingman actively served in politics. Vocally involved in controversial issues of the day with other opinionated, outspoken, ambition-driven colleagues in Congress, Thomas Clingman developed a reputation for being stubborn and persistent. He became one of the longest-serving congressmen in North Carolina history. During his seventh term in Congress, one of his lifelong dreams came true. On May 7, 1858, he resigned from the House to accept a Senate seat that had recently been vacated. When Congress adjourned on June 14, Senator Clingman returned home to western North Carolina. December would take him back to Washington. For now, though, a high mountain in the Great Smoky Mountains had captured his attention.

Exploring the western North Carolina wilderness had been a passion for most of his adult life. Mountain ruggedness seemed to symbolize his tough, robust and often abrasive personality. The boundless perseverance and determination that energized his challenging political debates also propelled him up rocky, rugged peaks.

Clingman's love for Appalachian scenery unearthed a deeper, more sensitive man not readily exposed to historians or to the public. In 1840, Clingman was given three hundred acres atop Asheville's iconic mountain-guardian, Mount Pisgah. For fifty years, his beloved, 5,721-foot-high "huckleberry plantation" provided respite and renewal. "Though one must travel twenty-two miles from Asheville to reach its summit…" he wrote, "its beautiful blue on a summer evening is sometimes changed into a rich, purple by the rays of a red cloud thrown over it at sunset."

Expeditions into the Black Mountain Range of the Southern Appalachians, about thirty-two miles northeast of Asheville, prompted a dispute with his former University of North Carolina professor, Dr. Elisha Mitchell. The burning question remained: who measured the highest mountain in the Black Mountain Range first? The unfortunate disagreement ended in 1857 when Dr. Mitchell fell to his death attempting to verify calculations. Mount Mitchell, the highest mountain in the east at 6,684 feet, now bears his name.

In September 1858, Clingman turned to the Great Smoky Mountains. He knew of a high, rounded mountain that was known by settlers as Smoky Dome. Seeking adventure and political escape, Thomas Clingman and his companions departed Waynesville, North Carolina, for the high Dome. For eleven tedious nights, "enlivened by the stories of the guides and their adventures in hunting," the team would camp on the Smokies' highest peaks, reveling in mountain scenery. Donati's comet appeared across the

Highest Mountain in the Great Smokies

"Domed" summit of Clingmans Dome as seen from Webb Overlook, Newfound Gap Road.
Photo by the author.

southwest skyline soon after sunset one evening. Personal pleasure and natural beauty were not the primary reasons for the expedition, however. Scientific exploration was. Clingman wanted to measure the height of Smoky Dome.

Joining Senator Clingman was Samuel Buckley, an avid botanist and geologist. Buckley was no stranger to the Southern Appalachians. Two years earlier, Buckley had explored the area with his friend, Professor Arnold Guyot, the scientist whom Clingman had hoped would join them on the present excursion.

Sixteen years earlier, Buckley and Ferdinand Rugel, a well-traveled field botanist, had collected botanical specimens in the Smoky Mountains. Leaving Sevierville, Tennessee, the pair had ridden by horseback up steep mountainsides. Preserving plants as they gained altitude, Buckley and Rugel rode up Alum Cave Bluffs Trail to the crest of Mount Le Conte. High-elevation forests intrigued them. Plant specimens, new to science, were collected and carefully packaged for the long ride out of the mountains.

On Mount Mingus near Road Gap, Buckley wrote, "We first met *Rugelia*...which has yet not been described in American works of botany." Buckley and Rugel frequently found the plant for twenty-five to thirty miles across Smoky's crest. A rare Southern Appalachian endemic, Rugel's Indian plantain *(Rugelia nudicaulis)* was named for Dr. Rugel, the German botanist. The scientific names of other high-elevation specialties, like Blue Ridge St. John's wort (*Hypericum buckleyi*), were given Buckley's name. Over their lifetimes, the pair would amass sizeable plant collections. Buckley alone would identify twenty-four new species and accumulate over six thousand specimens in his personal collection. His herbarium is now owned by the Missouri Botanical Gardens.

In his preparations for the 1858 trip, Senator Clingman also invited a friend and fellow politician, Dr. Samuel Love. Other men joined the expedition to help carry the heavy, cumbersome load. From Cherokee, North Carolina, the team followed the course of the Oconaluftee River. They packed in enough provisions for several days and extra gear for extreme weather, as well as two of Green's standard barometers. After climbing the steep terrain to an area near the current pass now known as Newfound Gap, Thomas Clingman reached the crest of the Smokies.

Bushwhacking slowed the ascent. Masses of gnarled, tangled rhododendron barricaded their route, like a moat protecting its castle. Samuel Buckley wrote, "The toil was great, and the difficulties to be encountered can only be imagined by those who have ascended the steeps of the unfrequented

Southern Alleghenies [Appalachians], through laurel thickets...and multitudes of the prickly locust, which has a penchant for scratching the face and hands, tearing the clothes, and occasionally the skin beneath."

Vigilant care guarded precious scientific instruments from unsteady footholds. Giant boulders interrupted a dense forest understory as they neared the top. Low clouds released raindrops clearing the broad, open skies. Great valleys spread beneath them, "and many a waving ridge, imitating in its curling shapes, the billows of the ocean when most lashed by the tempest," wrote Clingman in a letter to Professor Joseph Henry of the Smithsonian Institute. So enthusiastically verbal were his descriptions of the mountains that he felt the need to apologize: "Forgive me for this long letter...a trespass on your time."

Vast horizons rippled with long ridges and high peaks. Did Thomas Clingman recognize his Mount Pisgah perched on the most distant ridge forty-three miles to the east? Could he see "the angular eminence" of Cold Mountain, part of Shining Rock Wilderness that he had explored years ago? Later, Clingman would write in an article published in *Appleton's Journal* on December 27, 1878, that Shining Rock was "an immense mass of quartz so white as to resemble loaf-sugar...standing like an immense edifice of snowy marble."

No tower elevated Clingman above the treetops on Smoky Dome as it would today. Dense fir canopies limited his views. The inevitable, ever-present Smoky "haze" may have reduced visibility as well. Numerous nameless peaks rose around him. Did Clingman realize that the hump, barely visible to the naked eye, seventy-three miles away, was Mount Mitchell, whose tip-top rock was forty-one feet higher than where he was standing?

Barometric readings were taken on the Dome. Down in Waynesville, North Carolina, John Le Conte, a professor of physics and chemistry from South Carolina College, was observing barometric readings for comparison. Differences in valley and mountaintop readings, taken simultaneously, were used to determine a mountain's height. On the Dome's shoulders, to the east and west, sat two lower peaks. Their elevations were also measured. Buckley and Clingman were ecstatic. Preliminary records indicated that the Dome was higher than Mount Mitchell in the Black Mountains. They were standing on the mountain that was truly "highest east of the Mississippi"! Not until a year later would they learn that their calculations far exceeded the mountain's true height.

Their great discovery, "the highest mountain," could only have one name. Which man could claim the fame? Should Smoky Dome be Mount Buckley or

Mount Clingman? Celebratory enthusiasm degraded into conflict. Inflated egos, with each wanting notoriety, fueled a bitter disagreement. Reminiscent of the former Clingman/Mitchell debate, Buckley and Clingman aired their grievances publicly. In November 1858, the *Raleigh Register* printed Buckley's words that Clingman was ignorant of scientific observation. Buckley claimed that he alone had measured the mountain. Clingman's supporters countered in Asheville newspapers that the senator was responsible for the preparations and had supervised the expedition.

Back in May, Governor Thomas Bragg had given Clingman a temporary senate seat, a position made available when Senator Asa Biggs resigned. Now, the seat had to be earned. In November, in the midst of the bitter Buckley dispute, Thomas Clingman was elected senator from North Carolina by state legislators. In 1858–59, supporters proposed that a western North Carolina county be named "Clingman." However, party-line voting rejected the bill. In 1861, the county was named "Transylvania." Many years later, a 6,520-foot peak in the Black Mountains, near Mount Mitchell, now overly towered by radio transmitters, was named Clingmans Peak. How would Senator Clingman's name officially become attached to the great Dome of the Smoky Mountains?

In the summer of 1859, Robert Collins, a native mountaineer, welcomed Professor Arnold Guyot to the Great Smoky Mountains. As a guide arranged by Senator Clingman, Collins slashed, cut and moved thick underbrush ahead of Guyot across the high-elevation, rugged crest. Colonel Robert G. Love, of Waynesville, had loaned Guyot a horse, not because he was a tenderfoot but to bear his barometric burden, the most sensitive, up-to-date scientific equipment shipped from Paris. His horse, Guyot believed, was the first to reach the Dome.

Professor Guyot's meek, scholarly appearance disguised his tough grit. For such a small, articulate, brainy man from Princeton College, New Jersey, his physical accomplishments were astounding. In the mid-1800s, little of the Appalachian Mountains had been mapped or explored. Meticulous in his attention to detail, scientific in logic and precise with recording, Guyot started measuring and charting each of the major peaks, climbing them one by one. The year 1849 found him in the Northern Appalachians. By the late 1850s, he'd turned south. By age seventy-four, he'd measured all primary Appalachian peaks, north to south.

Born in 1807 in Switzerland and educated in Germany, Arnold Guyot followed his friend Louis Agassiz to America. After studying glaciers in the Swiss Alps and helping to create the United States Weather Bureau,

Professor Arnold Guyot (September 8, 1807–February 8, 1884). *Library of Congress.*

he dedicated his career to physical geography as a professor at Princeton College. In the classroom, he developed new curriculum and wrote numerous textbooks for children. During summer "working vacations," he put his vast knowledge of physical geography to practice: Professor Guyot climbed mountains.

His legacy, however, is not a lifetime of mountain climbing but of scientific study. His was a mission of topography and geography. In a letter to the editor of the *Asheville News*, published July 18, 1860, after his third summer in the South, Professor Guyot emphasized his purpose, stating that "my attention is far from being confined to the measurement of the elevation of the highest points, which is in fact of less importance than the physical structure, the proportion of all parts and the relative situation of the various chains composing it."

It was the summer of 1859. At Clingman's request, Guyot had come to the Smokies. Three years earlier, he'd explored the Blacks, including Mount Mitchell, and he'd measured the Balsams. His mission now was to not only measure major peaks of the Smokies but also to remeasure Smoky Dome. Mountain conditions made precise observations challenging. High mountains were encased in clouds; rain showered day after day. "My trip to the Smoky Mountains was long and laborious," he wrote. "Much rain; great distances; impervious forests, delayed me two months…the danger of perishing from exhaustion is by no means imaginary."

Measurements were taken and repeated. Simultaneous baseline barometric readings were obtained at both Asheville and Waynesville every half hour for two days before he launched his expedition into the Smokies. The difference between base numbers and high-elevation readings determined a mountain's altitude above sea level. Exactness was the aim; consistency, the key. Rising daytime temperatures affected atmospheric pressure, skewing the results. Observations, he decided, needed to be made at dawn and dusk. Therefore, Guyot camped overnight on every mountain he measured.

On top of ol' Smoky, diligence to detail seemed more crucial. He "encamped on the summit," Guyot explained, "…for twenty-six consecutive hours, the barometer being observed every half hour there and below at Mr. Collins' house, except from 9 p.m. to 6 a.m. The result was an altitude of sixty-six hundred and sixty feet above the level of the sea." The Buckley-Clingman reading the previous year had been 6,755 feet. (Official height today: 6,643 feet.)

Guyot thought their error had occurred not in barometric calculation on the summit but in the baseline reading obtained in Waynesville. Also,

Mount Buckley from Clingmans Dome Parking Lot. *Photo by the author.*

Buckley and Clingman had taken their reading during the heat of the day, increasing the margin of error. Most important, Guyot's measurement put to rest Buckley and Clingman's belief that they had discovered a mountain higher than Mount Mitchell.

Professor Guyot thought the highest peak in the Great Smoky Mountains should be named for Senator Thomas Clingman. "He was the leader of the party which made in 1858, the first measurement," he explained. But unlike Mount Pisgah, which stands alone at the end of a ridge, Clingmans Dome shares the stage with a mighty group. Like Mount Craig and Mount Gibbs, flanking the sides of Mount Mitchell, lower summits rest on the shoulders of the Dome. To recognize the two other prominent members of the original expedition, Guyot designated the western peak, next in height, Mount Buckley; the eastern one, he named Mount Love.

Guyot named many Smoky Mountain summits during his excursions; some designations, however, are no longer used. The mountain he named Mount Collins, in honor of his helper, is now Mount Kephart. Mount Collins,

Mount Guyot, Mount Chapman and Mount Sequoyah, as seen on November 30, 1935. *Courtesy of Albert "Dutch" Roth Collection, University of Tennessee–Knoxville Libraries.*

today, is four miles below Clingmans Dome, north on the Appalachian Trail. There, a popular trail shelter also bears his name.

Like a true gentleman-scientist, Professor Guyot didn't name a mountain for himself. But his friend Samuel Buckley did. Mount Guyot (6,621 feet), the second-highest mountain in GSMNP, rises seventeen air-miles east of the Dome. (Guyot measured it to be 6,636 feet, only 15 feet over the official reading today!) Although the Civilian Conservation Corps (CCC) built the Appalachian Trail over its western edge in 1935, no trail leads to its summit. Much like Guyot saw it, carrying bulky survey equipment in 1859, a tangled bushwhack is required. Early Smokies writer and park proponent Laura Thornborough wrote in her 1937 book, "If its wilderness you want, go to Guyot!" One of the national park's loveliest waterfalls, Ramsey Cascades, tumbles from its slopes.

A New Hampshire mountain is also named for him. Guyot studied the Appalachian chain far more than any other explorer in the nineteenth century and probably far more than any Appalachian Trail thru-hiker today. Befittingly, a mountain was named for him at both ends.

Guyot's map was the first precise, well-documented record of Smoky Mountain elevations, topography and place names. His southern map and manuscripts, though, had never been published. Frankly, they were lost. For decades, no one even knew they existed.

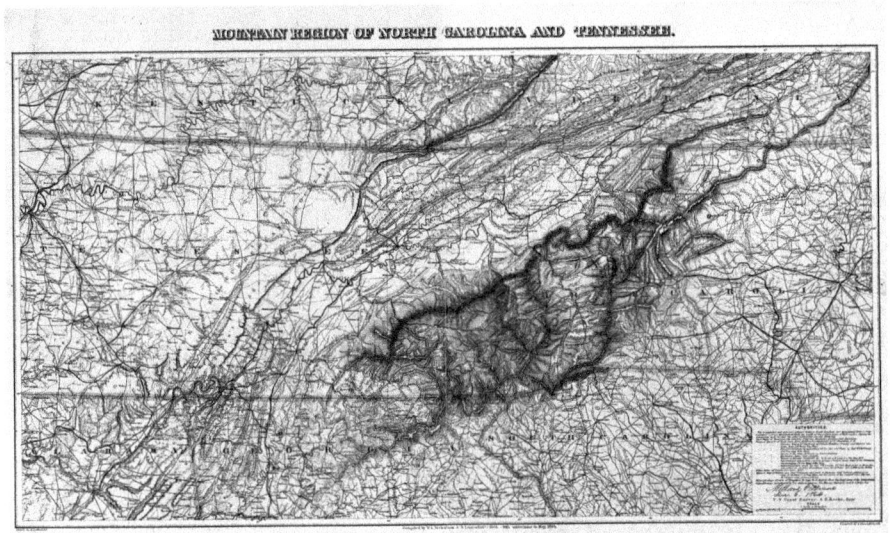

Guyot's map in the Millard Fillmore Collection. *Library of Congress.*

Uncovered under files in the Library of the Coast and Geodetic Survey, Guyot's map and manuscripts of the Smokies were discovered in 1929. Myron Avery, who tirelessly crusaded for the creation of GSMNP and the Appalachian Trail, found them while doing research. Today, the Library of Congress in Washington, D.C., stores a copy of Guyot's map from the Millard Fillmore Collection, signed by the thirteenth president of the United States on December 6, 1864.

Guyot provided a copy of his map to the Union military during the Civil War. His map depicted gaps through the southern mountains, names of the mountains, geographical relief and the location of Confederate roads and railroads. The route of a proposed military railroad was also included.

Within two years after Clingman's expedition in 1858 and Guyot's in 1859, the American landscape would make a dramatic change. The South seceded. The country was divided, and only a Civil War would solve the issues.

Buckley further explored the Southern Appalachians after measuring the Dome and then moved to Austin, Texas, to work as a naturalist/geologist. The Civil War found him in the North acting as chief examiner for the Statistical Department of the United States Sanitary Commission. In 1866, Buckley became Texas state geologist and remained in Texas until his death in 1884.

Arnold Guyot continued as professor at Princeton. Measuring mountains on his days off, he taught barometric techniques to geology students during his field studies. In 1862, he offered six lectures at the Smithsonian Institute on the "Unity of Plan in the Systems of Life." According to the *Memoir of Arnold Guyot, 1807–1884*, by James D. Dana, Professor Guyot lectured during the Civil War at Princeton Theological Seminary on the "Connection of Revealed Religion and Physical and Ethnological Science." Guyot continued to collect specimens for the museum he founded in 1856.

Like Buckley, his friend Guyot also died in 1884. Guyot Hall at Princeton is named for him. In addition to the two Appalachian Mountains, a Colorado Rocky Mountain bears his name. Guyot Glacier lies in southeastern Alaska. Guyot Crater dents the moon. The geological term "guyot," coined from his name, represents an underwater, flat-topped, extinct volcano, usually found in the Pacific Ocean. Besides his maps, charts, books and manuscripts, Guyot left a field toilet kit taken on mountain expeditions, now on display in Guyot Hall.

Thomas Lanier Clingman withdrew from his senate seat to become brigadier general of Confederate forces. Guyot's Southern Appalachian map told northern troops where to go, and Clingman's southern mountain knowledge told the South where to go to stop them. Although he sought desperately to regain his senate seat after the Civil War, President Andrew Johnson never pardoned him.

Postwar, Clingman unsuccessfully campaigned to be elected to a public office. His dream to become president of the United States would never be fulfilled.

A reticent recluse, though, he was not. Clingman endlessly lectured, wrote and publicly promoted western North Carolina's economic and educational development during Reconstruction. He promoted the local natural beauty and resources. Having discovered the first diamond in North Carolina in 1847 and the first platinum in 1848, Clingman advocated the region's mineral wealth. Clingman owned a zirconium mine near Hendersonville, North Carolina, and invented a lamp that used the chemical element. Clingman was instrumental in bringing the railroad to Asheville to connect his mountainous home to markets on the coast.

Although these commitments occupied his mind and his time as the decades passed, none of his projects provided much income. Strapped for cash at age eighty, Thomas Clingman was forced to sell his most prized possession, Mount Pisgah, for $800.00 to George Vanderbilt. He died in a state hospital in Morganton, North Carolina, on November 3, 1897.

Brigadier General Thomas Clingman pictured during the Civil War. *Clingman and Purveyor Family Papers #2661, Southern Historical Collection, the Wilson Library, University of North Carolina–Chapel Hill.*

Unlike John Muir of the Sierras or Horace Kephart of the Smokies, Thomas Lanier Clingman did not leave a diary or journal expressing his deepest thoughts or his internal sentiments. He chose to leave a collection of speeches and letters to record his life. He never married and never had any close family members to save personal items. Perhaps it is his proud, public presence that he wants us to remember. Perhaps he wants us to remember his commitment to principle and service, a voice for his people, his mountains and his country—a voice forever carried by the winds across Clingmans Dome.

CHAPTER 2

REMOVING A FOREST

In Paul Fink's chronicle of his camping experiences in the Southern Appalachians, *Backpacking was the Only Way*, he wrote on June 18, 1919, "Here at Balsam we encountered the first evidence of logging operations since we had left Mt. Collins. A great shock it was to us, to travel for days through a magnificent, truly virgin forest, where there was only the very faintest, scattered evidence man had ever been there before, and then step suddenly into the utter devastation the spruce logger leaves behind him."

On a hike on August 9, 1925, over Mount Collins near Clingmans Dome, he wrote: "Much of the valleys below us in North Carolina had been logged, the cutting frequently extending to the state line. This was also the property line between holdings of different companies, but we noticed that the timber companies were in no wise scrupulous in observing actual boundaries if a few choice trees stood just beyond. We did not pass through any areas of actual cutting, but at intervals could hear faintly the shrill whistles of the locomotives and steam skidders far below…"

By the early 1900s, northern logging companies had become interested in prize virgin timber growing in southern forests. In his writings, Senator Clingman's glowing words about magnificent hardwoods and the "massive pile of the great Smoky Mountains, darkened by its fir trees" caught the attention of lumbermen.

President Theodore Roosevelt, however, wanted to save them. Forests dominating the country's watersheds needed to be protected. Roosevelt proposed a national forest system. In a 1901 report to Congress, he promoted

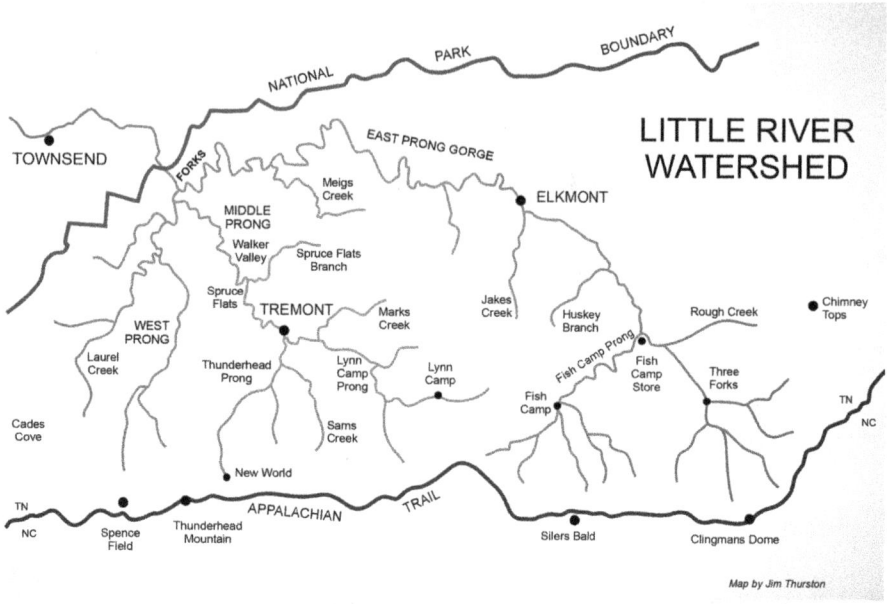

Little River Watershed. *Courtesy of Jim Thurston.*

Horse team pulling logs off Blanket Mountain. *Courtesy of Little River Railroad and Lumber Company Museum.*

protection of the Southern Appalachians, where some of the country's "finest and largest bodies of spruce" are found. Privately owned northern lumber companies moved fast before the government got involved. That year, approximately seventy-six thousand acres comprising the Little River Watershed were purchased, not to protect its waters but to harvest its trees.

Precipitation on Clingmans Dome supplies water to tributaries of the Little River Watershed of Tennessee. A logging company, eventually known as Little River Lumber Company, came to the Smokies to follow tributaries up steep Tennessee mountainsides to cut, slash and remove its trees.

Along the north border of Clingmans Dome Road, following the Tennessee–North Carolina state line, and across Clingmans Dome and Silers Bald to Thunderhead Mountain, the logging company's southern boundary was drawn. Its northern boundary stretched between Cades Cove and Gatlinburg. Logging towns with permanent buildings, stores and post offices were constructed at Elkmont and, later, Tremont.

Many locals became laborers for Little River Lumber Company. Harvesting logs was not new to them. Settlers had been cutting trees to provide fires for heating and cooking for decades. Trees were cut to build cabins, barns and wooden chairs. Horses or oxen pulled hand-greased tree trunks down steep mountainsides. Men loaded logs on wagons constructed from trees taken on previous hauls. In the 1880s–1890s, several small, family-owned mills operated in mountain coves to produce boards for local markets, as well as neighbors' use.

Little River brought newer mechanisms that offered improved, more efficient methods for removing timber. Draft horses were replaced by steam locomotives. Gear-driven Shay engines pushed railroad flatcars up steep inclines to skidder landing sites. Steam-powered skidders could reach high areas inaccessible to horse and rail. A skidder's long cables, J-hooked into large trunks, dragged logs down to loading areas. In some steep areas, intricate log chutes funneled cut trees down to lower terrain.

Repeated snags and overland snarls were frustrating, however. Time-consuming hang-ups prompted new ideas. Enter the Clyde overhead-cable skidder. Pulleys rotated, lowering hooked logs suspended from overhead cables from high summits, like dry clothes retrieved from an urban clothesline.

Steam log loaders stacked logs from huge, accumulated piles onto the railroad flatcars. Backing and braking down sanded rails to lower terrain, the slow-moving, powerful Shays delivered loaded cars to marshaling yards at Elkmont and other sites. Faster, rod-driven steam locomotives transported the load to Little River's sawmill at Townsend.

Shay "9" Engine at Fish Camp below Clingmans Dome. *Courtesy of Little River Railroad and Lumber Company Museum.*

Near the headwaters of Little River, on Clingmans' north face, the company built a spur rail line and a logging camp. Three Forks, the company's highest-elevation camp, provided temporary housing while the Dome was being logged. Once Clingmans' forest was removed, the portable buildings were reloaded onto railway flatcars and taken to the next work site.

Three small streams (Spud Town Branch, Kuwahi Branch and Grouse Creek) come together about one mile below Clingmans' summit, now National Park Backcountry Campsite #30, or "Three Forks." The primitive campsite can be reached by hiking the Appalachian and Goshen Prong Trails from Clingmans Dome or by hiking Little River and Goshen Prong Trails from Elkmont. Old logging and railroad relics can still be seen in streams and alongside the trails.

After thirty years of sawing, skidding and hauling away massive amounts of timber, Little River Lumber Company was the first to sell its land to the National Park Service. However, the first to sell was the last to leave. In exchange for accepting a lower purchase price, Little River was allowed to continue harvesting lumber for fifteen years after GSMNP was established.

Fish Camp store. A logging train veering right headed up Fish Camp Prong. The track curving left followed Little River up the north face of Clingmans Dome. *Courtesy of Little River Railroad and Lumber Company Museum.*

Last log cut by Little River Lumber Company. *Courtesy of Little River Railroad and Lumber Company Museum.*

A tulip poplar, hemlock and black cherry cut in Walker Valley at Tremont were the last three trees harvested. At Townsend's mill, teeth of a well-used band saw sliced each one. At 2:00 p.m. on July 5, 1939, the poplar was the last tree cut. Logging historian Bill Hooks reports that the mill whistle blew until no steam was left in the boiler, signaling the end of operations.

Twelve lumber companies logged two-thirds of the land that became GSMNP, of which 25 percent was located in spruce-fir forests. Three companies divided ownership of spruce-fir forests around Clingmans Dome. The holdings of Little River Company in Tennessee and Champion Fibre in Canton, North Carolina, covered, by far, the greatest area. Sandwiched between Little River and Champion, and the W.M. Ritter Company west of Silers Bald on Hazel Creek, was Norwood Lumber Company. From 1910–1926, Norwood's crew of four hundred men cut the southwest face of Clingmans Dome near the headwaters of Forney Creek.

Forney Creek, with one of the swiftest-flowing currents in the Smokies, amply supplied the water needed to produce steam for locomotives, loaders and skidders. With an elevation drop of almost four thousand feet in eight miles (from Clingmans Dome Parking Lot to the riverbed at the valley's floor), the Dome's rugged terrain presented some of the greatest logging challenges in the region.

A narrow-gauge railroad followed Forney Creek, climbing the watershed's steep grade. Switchback, zigzag routes eased the steady climb and helped brakemen control slower descents. Spur lines followed tributaries. Within a mile of Clingmans' summit, loggers removed its timber. Lands cupped between Welch and Forney Ridges were also logged. Sometimes "ballhooting" was practiced: men simply shoved huge trunks down rugged mountainsides, begging gravity to take over.

When Norwood's skidders and Shay locomotives could not provide access to the steepest regions, restricting the harvest of some of the best timber, Norwood devised another plan. Incline railways were constructed to access steep gradients. One climbed the south side of Clingmans Dome between Devil's Courthouse Ridge and Forney Ridge.

The incline route extended Norwood's narrow-gauge railroad line. Steam, generated by a huge boiler, powered heavy cables to raise and lower incline railway cars into deep ravines. A dense forest, covering a mountainside so steep that even the hardiest of men were challenged to remain upright, could now be harvested. Negotiating such steep terrain was impossible for draft horses. Simply shoving heavy logs downhill was impractical. Incline rail was not only safer but also much more efficient. Much the same way that

Norwood's three-foot-gauge, Type-A Climax Engine ("Black Satchel") with self-propelled American Loader, a rare early engine with two speeds: forward and backward. The wooden tub held sand for the rails. *Jerry Ledford Collection.*

a rescuer pulls stranded mountain climbers to safety, heavy cables tugged against weight and gravity to retrieve their prized load for transport.

At the confluence of Forney Creek and the Tuckasegee River, Norwood built its mill town. Forney had several sawmills to process lumber, as well as a store, school, church and homes. Here, Norwood's ten-mile railroad connected with the Southern Railway.

Downstream from Bryson City, North Carolina, founded in 1871, Forney was located in an area known for its lumbering history. Bushnell operated in 1879; Noland Creek was the site of a lumbering town in the 1880s. In 1910, Proctor was the mill town of Ritter Lumber Company, which logged Hazel Creek during the same period that Norwood logged Forney. All four mill towns are now lost to history; all, except Proctor, were submerged under Fontana Lake. R.E. Woods of Montvale Lumber Company built Fontana, a village for his railroad hub. Today, Fontana is a beautiful resort village. Kitchen Lumber Company's mill village was located near the present Twentymile Ranger Station.

CLINGMANS DOME

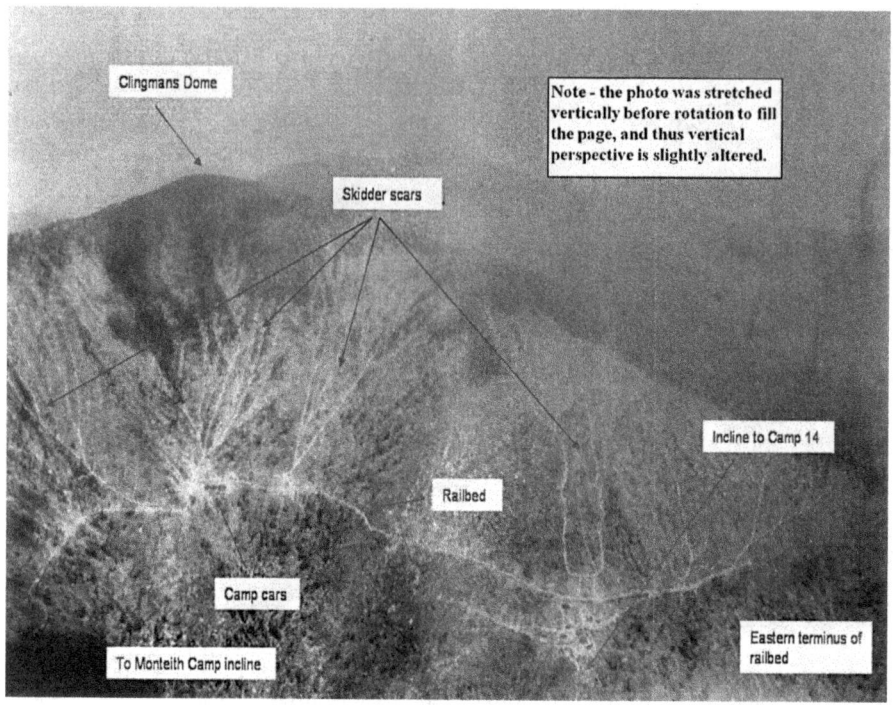

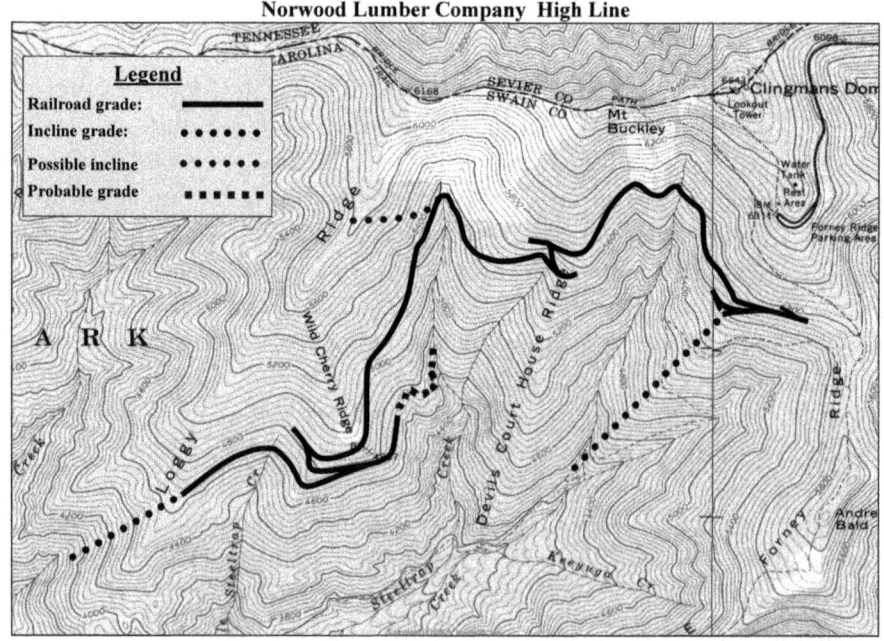

Norwood Lumber Company High Line

Above: Norwood's boiler and incline railway site below Clingmans Dome. Norwood's self-propelled American log loader is undergoing repairs in the left foreground. The boiler for its incline railway machine is right of center in front of the incline machine shed. Norwood's "Black Satchel," Type-A Climax locomotive is seen in the background, far right. *Jerry Ledford Collection.*

Opposite, top: U.S. Army Air Corps 1927 photo of Clingmans Dome, labeled by railroad historian/lecturer Ron Sullivan, detailing Norwood's operations. *Courtesy of Ronald C. Sullivan and GSMNP Archives.*

Opposite, bottom: Norwood Lumber Company's High Line. *Courtesy of Ronald C. Sullivan.*

Hike Forney Creek Trail from the Clingmans Dome parking lot. Both earthen scars and railroad relics recall memories of Clingmans' past. A severe fire in 1925, ignited by skidder, rail or engine sparks hitting dry brush, scorched miles of land up the sides of Mount Buckley and the Dome. Some charred trees still remain. See old railroad grades switchback up steep mountainsides. Bare gullies gouged by heavy logs shoved downhill by man or skidded off the mountain by machine are obvious. Camp where Norwood loggers did at National Park Campsite #68, about two miles from the trailhead.

Slowly, rock retaining walls, portions of old wooden trestles, iron railings, coal, parts of trains and logging equipment are being shielded from view

Norwood men at the commissary, Forney, North Carolina. Jerry Ledford's grandfather, Lois Ledford, is third from the left. *Jerry Ledford Collection.*

Norwood's Shay #1, Forney Creek, North Carolina. *Jerry Ledford Collection.*

A peeled chestnut log being loaded by Norwood Lumber Company. *Jerry Ledford Collection.*

by growth of vegetation and passage of time. Some say that the Forney Creek area contains the greatest number of logging artifacts in the park. Not far off the trail, shortly beyond the juncture of Forney Ridge and Forney Creek Trails, a huge boiler lies on its side. The boiler provided the steam for the incline machine that tugged railway cars over the steep side of Clingmans Dome.

Little River Company primarily cut yellow poplar, black cherry and hemlock. Massive, tall, straight-grained poplar provided excellent timber for building construction. Black cherry was scarce but highly prized. Giant hemlocks, some hundreds of years old, were cut and stripped of bark. Hemlock bark was in great demand for the tanning industry. Little River often left trunks to rot.

On its 16,983 acres, Norwood Lumber Company logged hemlock and hardwoods such as oak and chestnut. Norwood also wanted Clingmans' red spruce. Spruce was mostly in demand for paper. Clingmans' Fraser fir, yielding little pulp, was not favored. During World War I, the structural strength and light weight of spruce made it ideal for airplane construction.

The resonant quality of spruce made it perfect for musical instruments. A violin crafted of the Dome's finest spruce may still be tucked in someone's forgotten attic. Somewhere, perhaps, a Clingmans' spruce soundboard in a church piano has not warped and cracked, still producing notes as sweet as those of a winter wren.

Norwood Lumber Company's Superintendent Fatally Injured at Forney

By railroad and logging historian/lecturer Jerry Ledford, grandson of Louis Ledford. (Jerry's father was born at Forney.)
Superintendent Louis Ledford was replacing a drive belt in the planing mill during lunch break on Thursday, March 25, 1926. He was mortally wounded when the machine was turned on before he was finished. He was being transported to the Norburn hospital at Asheville on a special train that day and passed away in Canton, NC, while en route to the hospital. Louis was a brother-in-law to Louis Carr, one of the owners of Norwood Lumber. Part of the Norwood mill burned two days later on Saturday evening, March 27, and lumber operations at Forney were over.

Champion Fibre also preferred red spruce. Massive American chestnut trees were appealing, too. Establishing a pulp mill in Canton, North Carolina, beside a giant, healthy, virgin wilderness was an ideal arrangement, offering convenience, reduced transport costs and cheap land prices. In 1905, the Smokies had an abundance of both spruce and chestnut. Champion's ninety thousand acres included the headwaters of the Oconaluftee River, Deep Creek, Greenbrier Cove, Mount Guyot, Mount Le Conte, Chimney Tops, Andrews Bald, the eastern flank of Clingmans Dome and other lands.

American chestnut trees made beautiful white paper and provided huge amounts of bark for tanning operations. Champion's methods, however, were more productive, practical and cost-effective. Discarded trunks were turned into profits, not wasted. No longer ground up and cooked to extract the tannin, destroying valuable plant fibers needed for paper production, chestnut trees were thinly sliced. By shaving the chestnut to extract tannins, preserving the fibers for paper, proposed Oma Carr, an associate with Champion Fibre, one tree, processed for two purposes, multiplied profits.

Cabin on Andrews Bald, pictured September 18, 1932. *Courtesy of Albert "Dutch" Roth Collection, University of Tennessee–Knoxville Libraries.*

Champion's enterprise was huge. During its early years, the company was considered to be one of the largest pulp mills in the world. Champion owned its own railroad, the Tennessee–North Carolina rail line. Smokemont was its large, bustling mill village for loggers and their families, as well as a site for its band sawmill, edger and trimmer. In addition to its own giant logging operations, smaller logging companies contracted with Champion to cut and supply Champion with pulpwood. According to Wilma Dykeman in *At Home in the Smokies*, large companies, at times, even worked together to more efficiently remove timber: "Little River helped flume in spruce pulpwood to the Little River Railroad for shipment to Champion's paper mill at Canton, NC."

Below Clingmans Dome, Champion owned Andrews Bald on Forney Ridge, adjoining Norwood's timber holdings. Company officials considered having Norwood log Andrews Bald for Champion. If Champion had invested in a spur railroad line across its ridge near present-day Clingmans Dome Road, Norwood may have agreed. Champion, however, asked Norwood to consider transporting the pulpwood down to Forney Creek and loading it onto Norwood's flatcars. No agreement was ever reached, and the Andrews Bald area was never logged.

Naturally, when concerned citizens crusaded to have the Great Smoky Mountains protected as a national park, the largest landowner was the

Clingmans Dome

"Ballhooting" scars above Fish Camp. *Courtesy of Little River Railroad and Lumber Company Museum.*

most reluctant to leave. Champion wanted governmental protection of the Smokies as a new national forest, not a national park. Forest timber could be re-harvested over time, within policy, in a national forest.

The public was adamant. Only the protection by a national park was good enough for the Smokies. Champion wanted $9 million for its holdings. The company's demands included not only the value of the land, mill and railroad, but also its estimated value of virgin timber not yet cut. After extensive spruce-price research, negotiations and court proceedings, national park leaders reduced their initial counteroffer of $3 million to $1 million. During delays from bitter disputes, Champion threatened to intensify its timber operations. The plan was to take as much as it could before the company was forced out. A national park was coming. After three days of bitter—almost hostile—negotiations arbitrated in Washington, D.C., in April 1931, a mediated purchase price of $3 million was accepted by all parties. Mount Le Conte, Mount Guyot, the Chimney Tops, Clingmans Dome and other priceless acres would never see the saw of a logger again.

Logging companies were paid and left. Discarded equipment and debris were deserted. Unwanted limbs and crowns were tossed like garbage. Clear-cutting had left scars, barren land, eroded soils and parched vegetation. Approximately twenty logging fires had scorched the forests. Rich organic forest floor layers were sorely depleted. Ecosystems were disrupted. No restoration plan had been put in place. Hillsides were not reseeded or forests replanted. There were no land management or post-traumatic stress strategies.

Patience, perseverance and protection became the mantra. Long-term, gradual self-healing would eventually provide a healthy recovery. Nature's struggles would be overcome. Life was its purpose. Regeneration was just going to take time. And, now, the Great Smoky Mountains had all the time they needed.

CHAPTER 3

BUILDING A TOWER

Imagine standing on the highest summit in the Smoky Mountains in 1920. Like a child on a sidewalk, crowded with adults, eagerly looking for Santa in a Christmas parade, excitement wanes. "I can't see anything!" a small voice wails in his forest filled with grown-ups.

Tall fir trees would have hindered distant views from Clingmans Dome. Hundreds of seedlings, confined in close colonies, were as thick as velvet curtains. Low limbs overlapped. High branches almost connected. In a cloud or under an endless blue sky, the view was the same. Thick evergreen needles covered, concealed and consumed anything less than twenty feet tall. The push, scratch and scramble to the top provided solace and isolation, peace and relief, but little panoramic pleasure. An open bald or a rocky face would have offered sweeping views of the Great Smoky Mountains. But not Clingmans Dome. Not in 1920.

For generations, wildlife had foraged the Dome's forests. Dense firs hid Cherokee Indians in the 1830s from soldiers herding them toward the Trail of Tears. In 1858, Thomas Clingman's team chopped thick vegetation to claim the top. The year 1859 brought Arnold Guyot to the summit on horseback, following a hand-slashed trail. Pioneers hunted here, exploring the wild country. Botanists and early naturalists sought new specimens.

When war came in 1863, Union general Ambrose Burnsides and his troops took over Knoxville. William Thomas and his Confederate Cherokee Indian legions advanced to the high Smokies to secure the gaps. Clingmans Dome offered a perfect vantage point. Confederate soldiers could watch for military movement from an observation platform built on top of the Smokies' highest mountain. At Indian Gap, a few miles below the Dome, Cherokee soldiers carved a rough road across the ridge, providing a route for Confederate forces through the mountains.

Clingmans Dome and the high ridges remained wild and remote, however. By the early 1920s, Smoky Mountain rains had eroded the old road through Indian Gap. Heavy carts became mired to their axles in mud. Foot travel by man or beast was the only recourse. Paul Fink described a hiking trip to Clingmans Dome on July 22, 1927, saying, "A little foot travel and abundant rain had turned the soft woods-earth into a thick, sloppy black mire in which we often sank halfway to our knees...The top of the Dome bore as heavy a stand of spruce and balsam as we had ever seen. There was not a single spot from which to see out. The absence made little difference...for the cloud was still down around us...had the top been entirely bare, we couldn't have seen the length of a rifle shot."

What Fink did see on that trip was intriguing, though. Near the peak of Clingmans Dome was a crudely constructed, abandoned cabin, presumed by him to be that of a surveyor's party. In the late 1920s, surveyors built the first lookout tower on Clingmans Dome.

Susan Bratton, the park biologist who created Upland Field Research Lab, interviewed Carlos Campbell in 1975. Mr. Campbell, born near Mount Le Conte in Sevier County, Tennessee, in 1892, helped establish the Smoky Mountain Hiking Club in the 1920s. He and his companions hiked miles of backcountry wilderness. In Bratton's interview, Campbell described that first tower on Clingmans Dome, saying, "That first one... went up the corners in improvised steps...most people were afraid to go up...You just went through a hole in the floor of the thing and pushed yourself around. It was really dangerous."

Times were changing for Clingmans Dome and the Great Smokies. In 1926, President Calvin Coolidge authorized the creation of the Great Smoky Mountains National Park. Land acquisition began. Fundraising, surveys, purchases and, yes, court proceedings began in earnest. By the early 1930s, Tennessee and North Carolina had offered deeds to the federal government. The Great Smoky Mountains National Park was born on June 15, 1934.

Opposite: Surveyor's tower on Clingmans Dome, with a "Goodwill Tour" group at base on June 9, 1929. *Courtesy of Albert "Dutch" Roth Collection, University of Tennessee–Knoxville Libraries.*

Highest Mountain in the Great Smokies

CCC cutting timber to frame the wooden tower, October 1937. *GSMNP Archives.*

Much work needed to be done. People were coming. It would be necessary to open the gates to the wilderness, but maintain safety. Protect the resource, but make it accessible. Hard labor, long hours and extreme physical exertion would be required. But who was available to do the work? The Great Depression had hit, and FDR had a new idea, a New Deal. Send in the CCC.

The Civilian Conservation Corps (CCC) was created to help unemployed young men recover after the Great Depression. They needed the money, and public lands needed their help. Across the nation, CCC camps set up in national parks. About twenty-two dotted the Smokies, housing around two hundred men in each camp. Road and trail maintenance, bridge and building construction, rock walls and picnic grounds all benefited from their labor. Campgrounds, comfort stations and park headquarters were built. Nine fire towers were erected. And on Clingmans Dome, a wooden observation tower was raised.

A 1929 promotional brochure entitled "The Land of the Sky and GSMNP" stated, "Until government surveyors built a tower there, it was necessary to climb a tree to get a good distant view from this point on Clingmans Dome."

Framework of first section of wooden tower, October 1937. *GSMNP Archives.*

Climbing a tree and a surveyor's tower were unsafe visitor options, however. The CCC was there to make improvements. Using native materials, the CCC created a rustic, primitive observation tower to blend into the landscape. Established on May 25, 1933, on Newfound Gap Road between Newfound Gap and Cherokee, North Carolina, Camp Kephart, Company 411 (N-P Camp #5), was assigned to build it. By August 1937, excavation of the site had begun. Footings were poured with concrete, and framing timbers were transported to Clingmans Dome.

Work progressed steadily through September. For thirty dollars each month (twenty-five of which went home while five dollars stayed in the pocket), young men chopped, sawed and planed tree trunks with government-supplied hand tools. Tapered, trapezoidal framework provided four-directional stability. Diagonal bracing enhanced the foundation's strength. Single, sturdy, board-straight tree trunks steadied each corner. Fashioned on the ground, each side was raised one by one and bolted into place. Stripped, debarked and notched logs made smooth railings.

Zigzag steps rose between three platforms—two long, narrow landings inside the log framework, with an upper, open level "about the size of a living room," described Carlos Campbell. A visitor was lifted forty feet above the Dome for sweeping views of the Balsam, Nantahala, Unicoi and Smoky Mountain Ranges. Superintendent J.R. Eakins reported to the director of national parks, "[The tower was] designed for the visiting public to see over the tall spruce-balsam forest that completely covers the dome."

Completed railings, looking from the third level to second level. *GSMNP Archives.*

Highest Mountain in the Great Smokies

Visitors on the second level of the tower, completed in 1938. *GSMNP Archives.*

Extreme weather conditions halted tower construction in mid-November. A side camp, Camp Forney Creek (N-P #9), was created from the Camp Kephart crew. Located in the valley beneath Clingmans Dome, Forney Creek Camp, the first CCC camp in GSMNP, began operations in 1933 but had been abandoned in 1936. Now reopened to assist Camp Kephart, Forney Creek Camp was occupied intermittently until March 1938. Construction of roads, trails and rock walls continued until spring. During warmer 1938 weather, the tower was completed.

After tractor travel had ceased hauling construction material to the Dome, the CCC finished the Dome trail. Culverts promoted drainage, and shaped banks prevented erosion. Crushed rock packed the trail. A rock comfort station provided bathroom facilities. (In 2010, this historic building was restored as a visitor center with the aid of funds provided by the Great Smoky Mountains Association.) Stonemasons built retaining walls from locally quarried materials. By blasting solid rock, the parking lot was graded. Extreme cold and torrential rains occasionally hampered the progress. Work was dangerous. Rock slides were common. Injury was always a risk. A CCC man was assigned as night watchman at Clingmans Dome to guard the masons' valuable equipment.

Highway under construction at Indian Gap. August 12, 1934. *Courtesy of Albert "Dutch" Roth Collection, University of Tennessee–Knoxville Libraries.*

The "Land of the Sky and GSMNP" 1929 article also stated, "At present, until Federal highways are built into and through the Park, one can go in a car to Smokemont, on the Ocona Lufty River, then with pack horse or on foot to the crest of the divide at Indian Gap."

The CCC improved that too. Newfound Gap Road was built across the crest of the Smokies. In 1935, the "Skyline Drive," Clingmans Dome Road, was graded, ditched and surfaced for automobile travel. Five thousand feet above sea level, seven miles of roadway connected Newfound Gap to Clingmans Dome. Over one hundred pounds of native grass seed had been collected from Andrews Bald to reseed disturbed roadsides.

"Couple Wed Atop Tower on Clingmans Dome" was the title of a 1930s newspaper article. Seventy friends, in wedding attire, shuffled through a dusting of snow to the tower for the first wedding held on the Dome. On the top wooden platform, the minister stood with one foot in Tennessee and the other in North Carolina. The couple, however, huddled in the northwest corner. Their marriage license had been issued in Tennessee; to be legal, they had to wed in Tennessee. Guests crowded on the upper deck, but "so small [was] the space, it was impossible to picture…all together."

The new wooden tower was celebrated. Visitors came, with numbers increasing annually. The wilderness in the Smokies was closer than ever.

Wooden Clingmans Dome Tower, completed 1938. *GSMNP Archives.*

Then, there was war. World War II needed a few good men, and the CCC left to serve. In 1942, the Civilian Conservation Corps was disbanded.

Maintenance labor for the national parks during war years was unavailable. Funding was almost nonexistent. Routine upkeep was nearly impossible. Roads eroded. Mountains reclaimed trails. In some parts of the nation, public lands were even used as military training camps and hospital sites, severely impacting forested areas. Buildings deteriorated, and the wooden tower on Clingmans Dome was no exception. By 1950, the tower, no longer safe, was dismantled.

A postwar public, hungry for peace and pleasure, flocked to the national parks. Park service finances could not keep up with public demands. Overcrowding and overuse was reducing the quality of the natural resources the public wanted to protect. The national parks, especially the Great Smokies, were being loved to death.

In 1953, one passionate activist begged Congress earnestly: either do something about the serious decline or just close the national parks to protect them. Voices of conservationists, park service staff and the concerned public were heard. In 1956, President Eisenhower signed Mission 66, a federal program to fund the development and improvement of the country's neglected natural resources. Over ten years, Mission 66 would bankroll the construction of new visitor centers, campgrounds, roads, park headquarters, picnic areas and other tourist facilities. In addition to these needs in the Smokies, Mission 66 funded a new Clingmans Dome Tower.

Across the nation, the Mission 66 construction style was uniform. Emphasis was on simple design, enduring materials and reduced labor. A functional focus outweighed traditional craftsmanship. Contemporary designs were promoted over conventional ones. The world's attitudes, ideas and visions had changed since the Great Depression and the Great War. "Modern" European ideas had migrated to America. Rustic designs had become outdated and old-fashioned, even to the National Park Service. To protect the resources while providing services for growing numbers of visitors, the NPS followed the lead of American cities by becoming "modern." So did the Smokies. And so did the Clingmans Dome Tower.

A new observation tower was a priority with Mission 66 dollars, a tower that would withstand severe high-elevation elements, accommodate a large number of people and be safe for a wide range of physical capabilities.

Architect Hubert Bebb proposed a design to meet those needs. On many vacations, he'd camped in the Smokies, and he was fond of Clingmans Dome. To research the tower project, he assessed the topography, forests and views. Discussions with park officials and visitors led to sketch after altered sketch.

Finally, his vision for the tower was born from the forest itself. Fraser firs covered the Dome. Tall, smooth gray trunks rose shoulder-to-shoulder like proud armies guarding the summit. How could he design a massive sturdy structure that was functional, safe, cost-effective and long-lasting and yet minimally impact the beautiful, forested summit?

Bebb envisioned eight gray concrete columns, or "trunks," supporting a spiral ramp rising to a 45-foot-high observation platform. Taller columns near the platform reached thirty inches in diameter; shorter columns decreased in width. Rough surfaces mimicked tree bark. A 375-foot ramp, gradually climbing through the forest canopy, would complete a circle, 100 feet in diameter. Fraser firs would remain in the center of the spiral, reducing forest invasion.

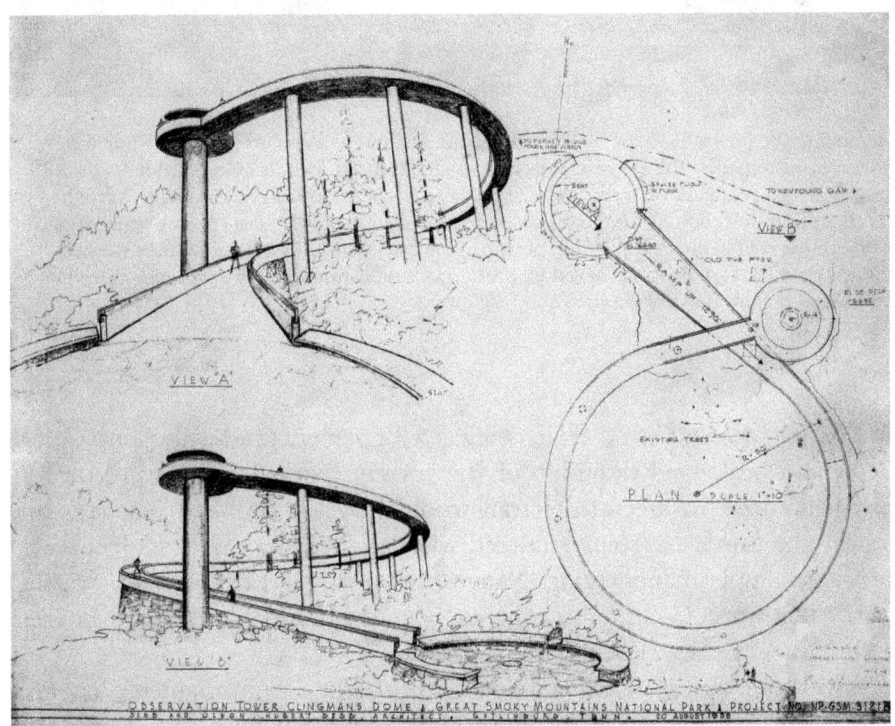

Copy of original blueprint drawings by Hubert Bebb, architect of current Clingmans Dome Tower, dated August 28, 1958. *Courtesy of Mountain Press, Sevierville, Tennessee.*

Removing the forms from the ramp and finishing concrete. With an innovative intellect, ahead of his time, Bebb's formwork design created a ramp with its own built-in "scaffolding," reducing materials, labor, costs and burdens on the environment. As each ramp section was completed, the forms were advanced. Completed sections became new work platforms for the next portion, pouring concrete section-by-section as they worked their way to the top. Bracing moved forward, too, supporting the new sections factored for additional height. *GSMNP Archives.*

Like Clingmans Dome Trail, rising at a 12 percent grade, the ramp would become a prolonged extension of the current hard-surfaced trail. Anyone physically able to ascend the trail would have no problem reaching the top of the tower. No steps hindered wheelchairs. The ramp, six feet wide, provided ample maneuvering. Native stone formed a circular patio at the ramp's entrance. Continuous concrete benches, bordering the patio, offered a "breather" before climbing to the top.

A covered observation platform, twenty-eight feet in diameter, opened above treetops at the end of the ramp. Supported by a round concrete column, eight feet in diameter, the circular level provided a 360-degree panoramic view.

This photograph shows the method of erection of cement pipes in the tower's main column. 1959. *GSMNP Archives.*

Hubert Bebb, architect (1903–1984). *Courtesy of Lee Mellor, Buckhorn Inn, Gatlinburg, Tennessee.*

Many architects offered proposals. But, by meeting Mission 66 architectural guidelines—simplicity in design, well-proportioned in structure, convenience of materials and low maintenance over time, as well as the overall tower appearance—Hubert Bebb's design was accepted by the National Park Service. A contract for $57,000 was awarded to W.C. Norris Construction Co. of Waynesville, North Carolina, to begin groundbreaking in December 1958. Inclement winter weather halted progress until the following spring. However, precast concrete portions of columns and the tower were formed off-site during the winter to accelerate assemblage come spring and to lessen the environmental impact at the Dome.

Loading sections of the main column at Clingmans Dome parking area. This type of truck was used to haul most materials. A small concrete plant operated at the top, and a tractor-driven cart hauled the concrete to the worksite. 1959. *GSMNP Archives.*

Conservationists were unhappy. Modernism, they said, had no place in national parks. Many preferred the traditional construction of wood and stone to harmonize with the natural elements. Concrete sidewalks and ramps did not belong in the wilderness. The proposed "Sky-Post" was too large and unsightly. It was too metropolitan and futuristic. The new observation tower would look like a UFO had landed on the Dome. Some wanted a conventional-style fire tower, similar to the wooden tower removed years ago.

Great Smoky Mountains National Park, like its sister parks nationwide, had entered a new era. Millions of visitors were coming to the "wilderness" for recreation, adventure, relaxation, nature study and escape. The high-paced, busy modern world prompted the need for souls to reconnect with their natural roots. Park service managers had a dilemma: How do we host so many people with a wide range of interests and needs, without negatively compromising forest, field and stream? How can we best stretch the maintenance dollars we are given? How can we provide the highest quality of service to the greatest number of people? How can we keep them safe? What investments of time, labor and money will endure the longest?

Opinions will always differ. Changing times will continue to foster new ideas. But one opinion voiced by Professor Maurice Brooks in his book,

A ranger-naturalist addresses the crowd at Clingmans Dome Tower in July 1961. *GSMNP Archives.*

The Appalachians, was shared by many: "No one will deny the need for an observation tower at Clingmans Dome. I have visited it when none was there; you reached the peak but you were so shut in by trees that you had little sense of accomplishment."

Climb Clingmans Dome Trail, rest a while on a bench and then slowly make your way to the top of the tower, winding above the treetops along the spiral pathway. You can even climb it in the rain; many do. Undaunted by the weather, Hubert Bebb cut a green ribbon across the spiral ramp leading to the tower at a rain-soaked opening ceremony on October 24, 1959. When he died, his ashes were scattered from the top of the tower. A local newspaper, *Mountain Press*, eulogized, "He's gone, but his vision lives on."

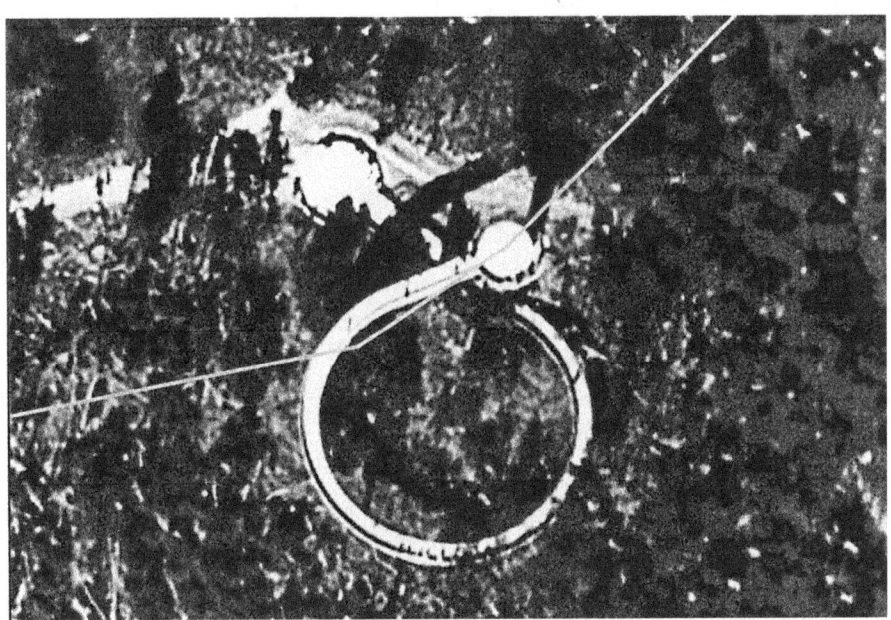

North Carolina–Tennessee state line across Clingmans Dome. TDOT bases the state boundary on the 1:24,000 USGS Topographic Map (Clingmans Dome NC-TN). The GIS referenced county (state) boundary was then placed on an aerial image background. *Image of the state boundary provided by the TDOT for this text, 2012.*

CHAPTER 4

EXPLORING AN ECOSYSTEM

Relationships are key. Survival often depends on them. Life alone, unsupported by a community partnership, can be fruitless and even fatal.

Flower petals advertise sweet nectar. Bees gather nectar to feed a hive. A bee's brushy body transports pollen to the next bloom, fertilizing it and producing a seed. A seed may be food for birds, or it may ensure the life of the flower's next generation.

A tree's canopy provides cool shade for plants that shun the sun's hot rays. Small mammals eat the tree's nuts; larger mammals eat the smaller mammals. Mingle and coexist, share and compete, adapt and change... together, plants and animals within an ecosystem contribute to the health and survival of that community.

The spruce-fir forest ecosystem in the Southern Appalachians is unique. Eighteen thousand years ago, a thick ice sheet covered Canada, extending in the east down to the Ohio River and Pennsylvania. Canadian vegetation moved ahead of the glacier. When temperatures warmed again, ice gradually receded. Forests followed northward, reclaiming their original homes. Northern plants migrated back to native lands. Some, however, stayed behind, establishing new ecosystems in the south.

Spruce and fir trees moved up to the highest slopes of southern mountains, where winters were bitter and summers were short. High-elevation ecosystems became "islands" isolated from their Canadian ancestors. Southern climate was warmer and wetter than Canadian boreal forests. The "new" southern spruce-fir trees grew faster and larger.

Isolation and adaptation evolved into a southern spruce-fir ecosystem, home to some plants and animals normally found in the north. Some are rare; others are found nowhere else in the world.

GSMNP represents one of seven southern areas with isolated high-elevation ecosystems. Spruce-fir forests exist in North Carolina on Grandfather Mountain, the Black/Craggy Mountain ranges (which includes Mount Mitchell, the highest mountain in the east) and the Plott/Great Balsam ranges. Find spruce-fir ecosystems at Roan Mountain, on the Tennessee–North Carolina border, and in the Mount Rogers area of Virginia. About 90 percent of southern spruce-fir forests are located on protected lands, and 75 percent are in GSMNP.

On ridges above five thousand feet in the Great Smokies, Thomas Clingman observed, "As the eye…sweeps [the landscape] it is arrested by" a dense stand of firs. Some believe that Fraser firs descended from northern Balsam firs. Left by glaciers to thrive alone in the south, Fraser firs adapted and developed into a new species. Short scales on balsam cones evolved into long bracts on Fraser cones, a trait separating one from the other.

Dark green fir needles, attached directly to twigs, are long and flat on lower branches. Higher limbs with male or female cones have shorter curved, upturned needles. Underneath, light green surfaces are grooved with two white bands. Blunt, notched tips feel soft. Female purplish cones with pale green bracts stand up, eventually turning brown and fading on the branch to release numerous seeds, leaving a small spike.

Fraser firs grow thirty to eighty feet high from a narrow root system. Shallow soils in high-elevation forests can be less than eighteen inches deep. Bedrock that close to the surface requires that roots grow horizontally. Heavy rainfall and melting snow penetrate and reach bedrock quickly, causing landslides and exposing rock. Fierce mountain winds and heavy layers of ice can topple trees, leaving a jungle of downfall debris.

Smooth fir bark is covered with whitish blisters, containing resin. Aging causes thicker bark, cracking into broad ridges. Moss frequently grows on its trunk. Witches butter (a fungus) lives on dying fir trees. Over 280 species of mosses and liverworts, like haircup, sphagnum and stairstep moss, are found in spruce-fir forests. Club moss, an ancient plant, carpets the floor, germinating from its dropped seed twenty years later.

Above 4,500 feet, Fraser firs are only found in the south. Between 3,500 and 5,500 feet, red spruce grows along the whole Appalachian Range. A 60- to 120-foot spruce tree can be three hundred years old. The exterior brown bark conceals the inner reddish tones. Solid, close-grained spruce was harvested heavily for airplanes, gum, paper and other purposes.

Short, sharp spruce needles set them apart from all other conifers. Spruce needles extend from reddish-brown twigs on tiny "pegs." Remaining on the branch after the needles fall, these raised leaf scars leave spruce branches bumpy, not smooth like the branches of the firs. Both sides of the needles are dull green. Bark is scaly, without blisters, and often has numerous lichens. Brown cones with thin, broad scales hang down from branches and later fall to the ground.

Spruce and fir provide the perfect home for one of the smallest tarantula-like spiders (0.10–0.15 inches long) in the world. On shady, north-facing rock outcrops or boulders, moist moss in well-drained areas make an ideal habitat for the spruce-fir moss spider. A preference for certain moss/liverwort species narrows its choice of habitats.

Ranging from light yellow to reddish-brown and lacking any abdominal markings, scientists use distinctive characteristics to identify moss spiders in the field. Long jaws protrude beyond its first body section (composed of the brain and thorax), and two long spinnerets extend behind the abdomen. Spinnerets weave a silky, tubular web between mats of moss and their rocky beds. While captured prey has never been found, wingless springtails, which share the thick moss, are the assumed diet.

Mating occurs in November. Seven to nine eggs, encased in a clear, thin-walled egg sac, are laid in June. Carrying the sac with its fangs, the protective female relocates the egg sac if alarmed. Spiderlings hatch in September.

The spruce-fir moss spider was first described by scientists in 1925 from specimens collected on Mount Mitchell. Decades passed before the species was identified again. After collecting samples of moss spiders on Clingmans Dome, Mount Collins, Mount Le Conte and Grandfather Mountain, Dr. Frederick Coyle of Western Carolina University published a paper in 1981 redescribing the species and providing insight on its biology and habitat. In 1985, Coyle studied and published an article on its mating behavior.

After discovering the moss spider on Clingmans Dome in the 1970s, Coyle continued monitoring the Dome's population. In 1983, a sizeable, healthy population was recorded. By 1988, however, sightings had become rare. Fraser fir forests on Clingmans Dome had become seriously infested with the balsam woolly adelgid. Dying trees reduced moss spider habitats. Status surveys in the 1990s documented a lone moss spider found on Clingmans Dome and one on Mount Collins. Dr. Coyle also observed marked population declines on Mount Mitchell during this time period.

In the late 1980s and early 1990s, a marked decline in moss spider populations was also noted by Dr. Joel Harp of Oak Ridge National Laboratory. Loss of habitat had become a serious concern as protective canopies creating cool, moist understories had declined. This was largely due to the balsam woolly adelgid, which killed acres of firs. Red spruce, another important shade tree, was being affected by air pollutants and began growing at slower rates. Areas previously logged left soils exposed to drying sunlight. Little organic matter remained to regenerate growth, and steep hillsides became vulnerable to erosion. Recreational activities also impacted moss spider habitats. In 1995, the spruce-fir moss spider was federally listed as "endangered." Its habitat was listed as "critical" in 2001.

Since listing, additional surveys have revealed new populations. "Lost" populations were rediscovered. In the late 1990s, status surveys were funded by the NPS, U.S. Forest Service and U.S. Fish and Wildlife Service. Healthy, reproducing populations were found on Grandfather Mountain. In a 1997 survey on Mount Le Conte (where, in 1926, moss spiders were first discovered in the Smokies), Dr. Coyle found healthy populations in four areas. Coyle estimated that five thousand moss spiders lived in the largest three sites. That same year, small numbers of thriving populations were also found within a half-acre plot on Mount Buckley.

In 1999, Coyle discovered the first moss spider on Roan Mountain. Twelve small, individual sites were mapped on Roan, but the total number of spiders was less than that on Mount Le Conte. Mount Mitchell's populations were thought to be extirpated. In 2004, Coyle extensively surveyed GSMNP. Previously, seven moss spider sites had been identified in the park. New surveys revealed fifteen locations, including one found on Mount Love, one half-mile east of Clingmans Dome.

More recently, from 2007 to 2009, Dr. Coyle explored a wider range throughout the high elevations of the Southern Appalachians, documenting thirty-one new sites with moss spiders and finding populations on thirteen new mountaintops. A population was discovered for the first time in the Plott Balsams of North Carolina. Moss spiders were also newly identified in Virginia on Whitetop Mountain and Pine Mountain. The known range of this species now expanded fifty miles north.

Glenn Taylor, GSMNP biologist, continues to survey the park's moss spider populations previously mapped by Coyle. In a two-year study beginning in 2010, in remnant and second-growth fir forests, thirty moss spiders were found. These results indicated a stable habitat with no serious decline noted in moss spider populations.

Fraser fir skeletons above second-generation firs near Clingmans Dome Trail. July 2012. *Photo by the author.*

Concern for the moss spiders' future has prompted a variety of conservation efforts, some with disappointing results. A 1992 captive-breeding program by the Louisville Zoo, hoping to raise moss spiders to return to recovered habitats, was not successful. Treatment measures to combat the adelgids have been relatively ineffective.

Perhaps other projects hold promise. University of Tennessee–Knoxville has initiated a moss-propagation study. Laboratory analysis has identified rock types and moss substrate of its habitat. Can the spider's preferred moss be collected, cultivated and transplanted to rock outcrops to increase its habitat?

Research is underway to determine the genetic health of individual populations and the species as a whole. Future conservation efforts may include developing cryogenic techniques to preserve the spider's genetic material and transplanting moss spiders to viable habitats of nonreproductive populations.

What does the next generation bring? Have second-generation Fraser firs developed a resistance to the adelgids, allowing them to provide adequate moisture and coverage for moss habitats? What other moss spider populations exist? Ongoing research and status surveys will offer a broader understanding of the moss spider's life history and, hopefully, the means to preserve it.

High-elevation forests provide habitats for other creatures, such as chipmunks and red squirrels. Competitors vie for spruce nuts. All year, throughout the day, scolding chatter warns invaders of the red squirrel's claim to this space. Mounds of cores and cone scales beneath a spruce also stake its claim. Green cones are often snipped, tossed to the ground and stored in wet areas to prevent them from maturing and releasing their seeds before the red squirrel, locally known as the "boomer," is ready to eat them. Berries are preserved under pine needles; mushrooms are hidden in stumps. Eggs of nesting birds are often tempting. Find the "boomer's" home in an old tree cavity or empty woodpecker's hole.

Woodpecker holes may invite Carolina northern flying squirrels (NFS). Southern flying squirrels live at lower elevations. Cavities are lined with shredded birch bark. Stick nests on conifer boughs, known as dreys, make cooler summer dens. Shy and secretive, northern flying squirrels glide—not fly—from branch to tree by night. Loose skin outstretched like a poncho between wrists and ankles holds them aloft. Descending one foot for every three forward-feet, the only way is down. To gain altitude, the squirrel climbs a tree.

Common in the northern United States, NFSs were first discovered in the upper Southern Appalachians in the 1950s at Mount Mitchell, Roan Mountain and GSMNP. No confirmed sighting followed for decades. The year 1985 found the squirrel on the "endangered" list. Then, in 1987, a biologist definitively identified a trapped NFS in the Smokies, releasing it at Clingmans Dome.

Nuts, bugs, tree sap, birds' eggs and lichens whet the appetite of a NFS, but fungi are favored. Fruiting bodies of underground hypogeous mycorrhizal fungi (truffles, false truffles, etc.) emit an irresistible odor to a NFS. By ingesting, and then dispersing, fungi spores across their home range, NFSs not only ensure its valuable food source but also provide beneficial fungi for red spruce growth.

A broader understanding of an endangered species promotes improved conservation measures. Winter nest box surveys as well as acoustic monitoring provided valuable information. Studies of NFS lifestyle led to habitat management. In 2010, genetic research suggested that North Carolina, West Virginia and Virginia northern flying squirrels were three distinct populations. Subsequent studies are planned.

Dr. Peter Weigl of Wake Forest University believed human impact on NFSs was an important consideration. Studies along a scenic North Carolina highway suggested possible fragmentation of the NFSs' habitat. The North Carolina Wildlife Resources Commission made a historic move. To help gliding NFSs cross Cherohala Skyway, south of GSMNP, to their frequent feeding grounds on the other side, wooden poles were erected. Fifteen months of video monitoring recorded many NFSs exploring the poles. Thirteen were seen, gliding from pole to pole, like little trapeze artists, to safely cross the highway.

Hairy woodpeckers take flight in fir forests, too. Conifer boughs may conceal the woodpecker, but its loud "Peek! Peek!" contact calls to other family members, and its too-fast-to-count territorial drumbeats announce its presence.

Several songbirds return each spring to Clingmans Dome. Nesting in fir trees, each species occupies a different level. Blackburnian warblers crown the top. With a flame-orange chest and yellowish-orange eye patch, blackburnians are a birdwatcher's pot of gold in a fir forest. His royal highness should reign on high. Males audition for a mate, building a nest in the firs' canopy. Lichens that resemble Spanish moss, called old man's beard, are gathered from fir trees to craft their nests.

Northern flying squirrels may also line their nesting cavities with old man's beard. As a flying squirrel food source, lichens are high in vitamin C and carbohydrates. Lichens offer a food option during bitter winters and can be a valuable source of water. They're good indicators of a healthy ecosystem. Very sensitive to air pollution, restricted old man's beard growth is noted when air quality is poor.

Save the middle branches for black-throated green warblers. One's bright yellow head, atop a gray body and white belly, can be seen foraging at spruce or fir branch tips. In hot pursuit of a fleeing insect, the warbler will dart out, catching it in midair. Black-capped chickadees feed and sing in conifers but prefer to nest in the soft wood of a dead yellow birch. Larger than its lowland relative, the Carolina chickadee, its song has a deeper quality. Visually, the two species can easily be mistaken.

Observe red spruce and Fraser fir from a distance. A triangular silhouette is obvious. Their symmetrical cone shape helps repel heavy snow during harsh winters. Fatty substances in the needles protect them like a car's antifreeze. Internal feeding tubes, with elongated chambers regulated by valves, create air bubbles in freezing weather. Air bubbles prevent food and water pathways from becoming one long, frozen icicle.

Dense, flexible branches protect a conifer's interior. Snow cannot accumulate there. Deer mice know that. Possibly the most abundant mammal throughout the park, deer mice, like the southern red-backed vole and the rock vole, prefer cool, moist environments in higher elevations. The darkest nights of winter will find deer mice leaving snow-covered tunnels to scurry up spruce-fir trunks looking for food. And a wise little owl knows that.

Northern saw-whet owls silently hunt for deer mice by night and secretly snooze on evergreen branches by day. An owl's talons may find the mice along moss-covered stumps and rocky crevices. The size of a robin, the saw-whet is one of the smallest owls in North America. Hard to spot, they can be heard frequently in breeding season from February to April near the Spruce-Fir Nature Trail along Clingmans Dome Road. Count its one-syllable, regularly spaced, evenly toned vocal notes. Lonely males may serenade up to 120 notes per minute.

Find red-breasted nuthatches in middle spruce-tree zones foraging with chickadees. In large groups, nuthatches walk up, down and around trunks looking for food. Search conifer cones. Tiny nuthatches often hang upside down, prying out seeds. Like chickadees, they prefer a yellow birch home. Brown creepers climb up tree trunks, drop to the base and start climbing again. Under an overhanging piece of bark on the side of a tree, find its unusual but protected nest. Broader tree trunks with loose, peeling bark are favorite creeper playgrounds.

Scan branch tips for nests of tiny golden-crowned kinglets. A palm-sized cup, lined with moss, rests there each spring. A breeder in the high Smokies, kinglets may remain near Clingmans Dome throughout the cold winters.

Another small bird, the winter wren, sings from an exposed perch. Vocally gifted, its endless chorus of notes, trills and whistles is impossible to ignore. Dr. Fred Alsop, professor of biology at East Tennessee State University

Road Prong Trail to Indian Gap, as seen on February 22, 1947. *Courtesy of Albert "Dutch" Roth Collections, University of Tennessee–Knoxville Libraries.*

(ETSU) and author of *Birds of the Smokies*, writes, "The Winter Wren's long energetic song is one of my favorite sounds of the high, Canadian-zone forests. In summer, walk out one of the many trails in the spruce-fir forests and find a comfortable, moss-draped log to sit on. These are silent forests;

but as you sit quietly for a few minutes you will almost surely be rewarded by the rich smells of the conifers and the marvelously long, melodic song of the Winter Wren."

Preferring conifer forests, blue-headed vireos are the only vireos found near the Dome. Needles cushion their eggs in well-formed nests, often in rhododendron thickets. Besides beetles, bugs and caterpillars, these birds dine on the fall berries of mountain ash trees.

Black-throated blue warblers occupy lower branches. Add a white wing dot, and the name perfectly describes the male. Nesting in dense undergrowth, nests are seen at eye level by a child. Its lazy song may drift from higher perches when other birds have chosen to remain silent.

Combined totals of rain, snow, ice and mist drenching Clingmans Dome can equal eighty-five inches a year. Clouds cloak the Dome 25 to 50 percent of the time. Rock walls almost constantly seep groundwater. Plants and animals must adapt to a cool, moist, shady forest floor. Strong winds, changing in frequency, direction and speed, challenge the hardiest. Growing seasons are short; food sources are often scarce. There is less plant diversity here than in lower-altitude, hardwood forests.

Soil is so acidic that few earthworms live at this altitude. Freezing temperatures and extreme acidity slow the rate of decomposition and decay. Microorganisms cannot work as quickly as they do at lower elevations. Leaf litter and debris in a deciduous forest can decay in a year or so. Here, conifer needles may take up to ten years. Undecomposed conifer needles on the damp floor form a spongy mat.

Throughout the park, 140 species of snails live in damp leaf litter. One endemic species, found only in GSMNP, prefers spruce-fir forests. The one-inch-wide *Mesodon altivagus*, or "wandering globe," has a thin tannish shell of five to six whorls, often sporting a brown band on each whorled crest. Lungs, not gills, allow it to breathe air. John D. Slapcinsky of the Florida Museum of Natural History found this snail more common on Clingmans Dome in the 1980s. After a rain shower, he said, "It was difficult to avoid stepping on them."

Air pollution and canopy loss have affected their habitat. The death of mature Fraser firs has opened up hillsides to warm, drying rays of sunshine. Acid rain has increased nitrogen levels in the soil. Excess nitrogen leaches out minerals like calcium carbonate, which snails need to build their shells. Snail shells are a source of calcium for other creatures up the food chain. Animals such as salamanders, turkey, grouse and some songbirds feed on snails. This calcium supplement can be critical for birds to develop strong eggs and healthy nestlings. If you find a snail shell with a hole at the top, most likely, a mole or shrew sucked out its soft, fleshy parts for dinner.

In 2012, Susan Sachs, education coordinator at Appalachian Highlands Science Learning Center in GSMNP, reported that "citizen scientists" were monitoring changes in range and density of the *Mesodon altivagus* and other snail species. Most snails in the park have a calcium-based, rigid shell. One high-elevation snail species does not. With a flexible shell made mostly of protein, the *Vitrinizonites latissamus* does not require calcium from the soil. Information is being collected to determine whether its range is expanding under calcium-depleted conditions for which it is better adapted.

Among the mossy mats, mountain wood fern, intermediate wood fern and southern lady fern grow in profusion. Lichens living on rocks gradually build new soils. Abundant lichens (algae and fungus) are also found on tree trunks.

Of the thirty-one species of salamanders in the park, thirteen inhabit higher elevations. The red-cheeked, imitator and pygmy are the most common. Found only in the Smokies, red-cheeked salamanders live under rocks and logs. Red cheeks remind predators of their foul taste. Crafty imitator salamanders copy the red-cheek's facial mask to fool their enemies. No larger than a two-inch rubber band, dark-brown, inverted "Vs" line the backs of light-brown pygmies. Found only in eastern Tennessee and western North Carolina, the pygmy, one of the world's smallest salamanders, was first discovered in 1936 on Mount Le Conte.

Like all amphibians, a salamander's smooth, slick skin must stay moist. But, unique to the vertebrate world, these salamanders have no lungs or gills. Water molecules transport life-sustaining oxygen to the salamander's skin. Oxygen is then absorbed through their wet skin by a network of capillaries. Dry skin suffocates them. Frequent, misty air bathing Clingmans Dome provides a watery paradise. Burrowing in cool earth by day, salamanders roam each night, consuming hundreds of insects.

At high elevations, Virginia opossums, birds and bears feed on salamanders. Masked shrews and Smoky shrews are also sacrificed for hungry predators, but long-tailed shrews are more common on higher summits. Long-tailed weasels, red foxes, coyotes and snakes feed on shrews. Snakes are less common at five thousand feet, but black rat snakes and timber rattlesnakes may venture up in summer.

Snakes, raccoons, skunks and owls may feed on bats. Of the forty-six species of bats in North America, eleven live in GSMNP. All eat insects. A few inhabit higher elevations. Although bats have good eyesight, echolocation aids navigation and feeding. Their sonar capabilities are so sensitive that bats can detect an object as thin as a strand of hair. Although its frequency is too high for the human ear, differences in sonar calls, like bird songs, can identify an individual bat species. With a radar-like trait, bats track insects, trapping them in their tail and wing membranes. Nodding forward, teeth grab imprisoned prey dozens of times each night.

Most bats in the Smokies hibernate during winter when insects are gone; three species migrate. One hibernator in the colder high elevations of the park is the eastern small-footed bat. One of the smallest bats in the United States and one of the rarest in GSMNP, the small-footed is not often seen. Roosting in rock crevices in summer, they hang singly in colder caves all winter.

A migrating species is the rare silver-haired bat. Its fluttery, acrobatic flight is distinctive. Breeding in its summer range north of the park, it migrates south in winter. In the Smokies, silver-hairs roost in woodpecker holes, under tree bark and in hollow trees at all elevations.

One of the largest, showiest bats in the park also inhabits all elevations. Long, dark brown fur identifies the big brown bat, which may occupy buildings during the summer. Colder caves and hollow trees provide winter dens. Another summer home-invader, the little brown bat prefers warmer, lower elevation caves for hibernation. A hibernating bat's heart rate slows from one thousand beats per minute in summer flight to one to two beats every few seconds. The only endangered bat species in the park is the Indiana bat.

Unfortunately, in 2010, a little brown bat collected from its hibernating site in the Smokies' White Oak Blowhole Cave was diagnosed with White Nose Syndrome, a fungal infection that has killed over five million bats in the northeast. Caves in GSMNP were closed to the public. Scientists fear that unless they can learn more about the spread of this disease quickly, the little brown bat may be extinct in less than sixteen years.

Nocturnal, secretive bobcats inhabit Clingmans Dome but are rarely seen. Rodents and eastern cottontail rabbits, found at all elevations, are their favorite meals. Raccoons also wander throughout the park eating berries, reptiles, birds and small mammals. Groundhogs and white-tailed deer may browse high open areas but prefer lower valleys.

Avian ground dwellers include the dark-eyed junco and veery. The ever-present, under-your-feet, on-the-trail junco seems to own the place. It strings together a bell-like song from an evergreen perch. A mad "Chip!" and a bold flash of its white-bordered tail warns a foot too close to its nest. Come winter, it will choose to make an altitude adjustment or just stay near the Dome and brace for the bitter elements. The dark brown veery is difficult to see, foraging in deep leaf litter. However, its unique flute-like song sung from a high perch is unforgettable. A human soul rests when it sings.

Flocks of wanderers visit the Dome on a whim or when berry and nut harvests are plentiful. Cedar waxwings feed on holly and serviceberry at lower elevations but fly to the Dome to gorge on pin cherry and mountain ash berries, occasionally picking a single berry and passing it beak-to-beak to companions. Foraging in large, energetic flocks, the waxwing's short, repeated whistles suggest busy traffic cops on a congested London street. Atop a fir's pointed peak, a single waxwing, with masked face and raised crest, displays the colors of royalty. Dignified and poised, red "waxed-tipped" flight feathers and a yellow-dipped tail accent his warm brown body and pale yellow belly.

Sporadic flocks of pine siskins congregate in continuous chatter on red spruce trees, devouring their nuts. Find them feeding with nuthatches, creepers and chickadees. From 1936 to 1955, Arthur Stupka, the park's first naturalist, compared siskin visits to those of erratic red crossbills. Months that showed high totals of siskins indicated low numbers of crossbills. Both species, Stupka noted, could be found at all elevations any time of year. Pine siskins, however, seemed to prefer the Smokies in April. Red crossbills chose August and September.

The red crossbill's curved bill pries open conifer cones. Its extended tongue then lifts out the seed. Crossbills eat seeds of hemlock and yellow poplar trees at lower elevations. Pioneers reported crossbills pecking salt blocks left for grazing cattle. Civilian Conservation Corpsmen observed crossbills eating discarded rock salt, tossed after making ice cream. Today, Appalachian Trail hikers see them outside Silers Bald and Mount Collins trail shelters. Listen for their series of clicks and whistles at Clingmans Dome Parking Lot.

On April 19, 1938, at Indian Gap on Clingmans Dome Road, Stupka observed a male red crossbill with a grayish, heavily streaked companion. A short tail and uncrossed bill confirmed his suspicions: a fledgling crossbill, a first sighting that suggested that crossbills may breed here. Crossed beaks develop several weeks after leaving the nest. Their breeding history within GSMNP remains uncertain.

Consider yourself lucky if you spot an olive-sided flycatcher, a lone sentinel on some high, bare spruce branch. Its only companion would be its mate. Habitat loss, however, has reduced its breeding success in the Smokies. According to National Park Superintendent J.R. Eakin, "the most remarkable bird sighting" occurred on September 21, 1937. Two birders from Ohio State Museum spotted three white pelicans flying two hundred to four hundred feet above Clingmans Dome.

For years, downfall, disease and death have created gaps in coniferous forests. Disturbed areas permitted a flood of sunlight, warming the understory and drying out soggy soils. Hardy, high-elevation hardwoods like pin cherry, yellow birch, mountain maple and mountain ash have taken root. Brambles, such as thornless blackberry, and sprawling shrubs, like purple-flowering raspberry, spread quickly.

Some birds benefited from the spruce-fir forest decline. American robins, eastern towhees and gray catbirds, which normally occupy lower elevations, found new homes here. Shrubby areas are favorites for chestnut-sided and Canada warblers. Listen to the chestnut-sided; it's "pleased, pleased, pleased…to meet-cha!" Nesting on the ground under thick shrubs, the tame Canada, with its black necklace adorning a bright yellow chest, is a congenial host as well. Watch overhead at Clingmans Dome for hawks during fall migration.

Long, broad, jet-black wings lift a northern raven silently above the landscape. Soaring like an eagle, with a four-foot wingspan, its wingtip feathers move like individual fingers, adjusting to invisible air currents and eddies circling off high mountain ridges. Only its strange, croak-like call interrupts the sense of dignified freedom.

Low clouds that often drape Clingmans Dome are used to its advantage. Silently sailing through the misty cover, like a saw-whet owl uses darkness, the raven preys on unwary mammals, birds or whatever he can catch, dead or alive. One of the few birds known to survive Arctic winters, the raven's size, strength and stealth allow him to endure extreme high-elevation elements that others can't. Soaring over the Smokies, it scans conifer trees and rocky cliffs for a place to build its nest of sticks and bark.

What will survive the generations with the hardy raven? In its forest below, Fraser fir skeletons stand as blatant reminders. Fir seedlings offer hope. Unable to relocate, moss spiders cling to remnants, needing a little more space. Mosses soak up available moisture like sponges, while lichens hang on, craving a breath of fresh air.

Some vegetation dies; sunrays beam like spotlights. What was dark becomes light; wet becomes dry. Cool is now warm. The faded old opens opportunities to the eager new. New birds arrive to nest. Neighbors sing nearby. Plants better suited to changes endure. What adapts? What succumbs? What evolves with new survival gear?

Marooned salamanders, beetles and other insects thrive in a dwindling spruce-fir ecosystem. Others need them for sustenance. Stiff stems weather winds, waiting for pollinators to control their destiny. Are some insects specific pollinators for wildflowers that only grow here? If they are lost, can another creature take their place or do the flowers go too? Do others in the ecosystem rely on them for their own survival?

Southern spruce-fir forests have been rated the second-most endangered ecosystem in the country. Threats to this fragile region include balsam woolly adelgids, recreational development, previous logging and fires, climate change, habitat decline and canopy loss. Reduced gene pool in an isolated, fragmented community is a concern. Air and water pollution are major factors.

Cohabitate and support, endure and persevere, survive…What will survive to live with the raven?

CHAPTER 5
HOSTING AN UNINVITED GUEST

The year 1983 was eventful. A suicide bomber in a truck rammed a U.S. military base in Lebanon, killing two hundred marines. A South Korean jet carrying 269 passengers was shot down by Russians. The first American woman and the first black man flew into outer space, on separate missions, aboard the spaceship *Challenger*. President Reagan designated Martin Luther King Day. Cabbage Patch Kids, camcorders and compact discs were introduced, and a French scientist identified HIV. And, in 1983, on Clingmans Dome, aliens were discovered, changing the Dome's landscape forever.

The balsam woolly adelgid (BWA) *(Adelges piceae)* had entered North America almost eighty years earlier. Migrating from native silver fir forests *(Abies alba)* in central Europe, presumably clinging to firs transported to North American nurseries, the insect is thought to have first arrived in southeastern Canada. In 1908, the adelgid was discovered in Brunswick, Maine.

Any "true fir" belonging to the genus *Abies*—characterized by evergreen needles, erect cones and a triangular-shaped tree—can become the adelgid's new niche. In New England forests, adelgids no longer had access to their preferred silver firs. Balsam firs *(Abies balsamea)* became their alternate food source.

By 1928, adelgids were identified near San Francisco on exotic fir trees transplanted for landscaping. By the early 1950s, the insect was found in the Cascade Mountains of Oregon and Washington and later in the fir forests of Idaho and British Columbia. Pacific silver firs (*A. amabilis*), subalpine firs (*A. lasiocarpa*) and grand firs (*A. grandis*) whet the appetites of western adelgids.

No fir forest, however, was as devastated by the invasion of the uninvited guests as the Fraser fir (*Abies fraseri*) forests of the Southern Appalachians. Shenandoah National Park in Virginia witnessed its first adelgid outbreak around 1956. The pest began feeding its way down the crest of the Appalachians. In 1957 in the Black Mountains of North Carolina, adelgids were identified on Mount Mitchell. Three years later, an aerial survey revealed that two hundred thousand mature Fraser firs had died.

The invasive insects had found a gourmet diet: mature, solid stands of healthy Fraser firs. By 1963, BWAs had not only been found on Mount Rogers in Virginia but also in eastern GSMNP. Rangers spotted dead firs on Mount Sterling during a standard surveillance flight.

Like children unleashed in a candy store, adelgids fed with carefree abandonment. Few enemies or limits restricted them. Some predators were there; a few species of spiders and spider mites and an occasional insect-eating bird snatched some. Adelgids, however, were not their main diet. Approximately 241 other insects are known to inhabit Fraser firs. Warblers and others had many food choices. Huge quantities of adelgids, therefore, were not consumed by their few predators. Dense stands of old growth, mature Fraser firs that had crowned high southern summits for decades stood helpless, susceptible to unchecked, highly reproductive aliens.

Fraser firs responded, though. Innate security systems were initiated. When adelgids found weakened cracks in tree trunks and branches, their feeding tubes (stylets) pierced the rough bark, injecting a toxic saliva before sucking up food from the tree's sap. Like the human allergic reaction to spring pollen, firs overreacted. Excess numbers of abnormal cells were produced to build a wall around the wound.

Insult added to injury. Localized reactions caused fatal, systemic results. Compacted wood with thick walls clogged vital canals transporting water, sugar and nutrients from roots to crown. Just as a blood clot reduces blood flow through an artery, accumulation of abnormal cells blocked critical pathways. Food and water could not reach fir needles. Food production stopped. Growth halted. Within two to seven years, the Fraser fir starved to death.

The congregation of abnormal cells at buds and nodes along fir limbs caused excess swelling. Discolored needles dropped. New needles wouldn't form. Branches would stiffen and die. Heavy infestations of adelgids, sometimes as many as one hundred to two hundred adelgids per square inch and over fifty thousand living on one tree, hastened a fir's decline. Ironically, the Fraser fir's resin, often drained by early settlers into small containers through turkey quills to make a poultice for external wounds, could not heal its own wounds from the balsam woolly adelgid.

Adelgids fed aggressively in new stands of old forests. Wind, birds and other creatures spread the wingless insects to new locations. From Mount Sterling, BWAs advanced across the high peaks of the Smokies. The national park's management plan to clear-cut thousands of fir trees on Mount Sterling detained the advance but couldn't prevent it. By 1964, trees above Cataloochee were invaded. The year 1966 found BWAs on Mount Guyot on their way to Mount Le Conte. Proactive measures were set in motion. Research and monitoring were imperative.

The future of Clingmans Dome looked bleak. The range of BWAs was spreading across the high summits of the Smokies. In 1978, Dr. Ronald Hay, associate professor at University of Tennessee–Knoxville, had completed a two-year adelgid study in GSMNP. At that time, no adelgids had been identified in the spruce-fir forests of Clingmans Dome. One of his graduate students assisting in the research, Kristine Johnson, now works as supervisory forester for GSMNP. She has been monitoring and defending Fraser firs against the invader for over thirty years. During her tenure, she has watched BWAs repopulate, spread and consume over 90 percent of the park's mature Fraser firs.

Like Savannah waiting for General Sherman's Civil War "March to the Sea," the Dome was doomed. Defending the Dome from the inevitable invasion was an impossible dream. In 1983, when spruce-fir forest ecosystems were recovering from decades of logging and the abuse of man, Clingmans Dome was under attack, this time, by an enemy no larger than three grains of salt.

A concerted effort to win at least one battle by saving the Dome's valuable ecosystem became an urgent mission. Clingmans Dome was more accessible than other remote, infested fir forests in the park. Equipment and man could reach the Dome repeatedly to treat, monitor and follow up. The national park's accessible Balsam Mountain Road was also chosen as a treatment site.

In other areas of the Southern Appalachians where invaded fir forests were maintained by the U.S. Forest Service, predator beetles from India and Pakistan had been introduced. The results were disappointing. Chemical sprays were also undesirable alternatives. Inhabitants of valuable watersheds flanking Clingmans Dome could be seriously affected. Park officials chose an organic, biodegradable option: an effective insecticidal soap created by Canadian scientists in 1975. Potassium salts in the fatty acid soap broke up the BWAs' protective waxy outer shell. Death was certain. Made from plant and animal oils, organic insecticidal soap would pose no risk to humans or the environment. Disintegrating in about seven days, the soap left no residual, negative affect. Watersheds guarded by the Dome would not be poisoned.

Application was labor-intensive, however. The convenience of aerial spraying wasn't an option. Both sides of the tree had to be soaked and all surfaces thoroughly coated. Beginning in 1985 on Clingmans Dome and continuing for fourteen years, high-pressured water hoses mounted on modified fire trucks delivered powerful soap-sprays into deep cracks where the tiny insect fed. The underside surfaces of needled branches and the protected crevices of bud scales were other favorite feeding sites. Two hundred pounds of pressure drenched the insect's deep hiding places.

Two rangers could treat about an acre of firs in half a day. In July and September—when adelgids were at their greatest numbers and most susceptible to the insecticidal soap—man, hose, truck and spray coated nine acres of fir atop Clingmans Dome. A mixture of 2 percent soap and 98 percent water could also be sprayed by portable tanks.

From Mount Collins Gap to the Dome parking lot, Fraser firs lining Clingmans Dome Road were drenched. Trucks then climbed the paved, wide hiking trail to the Dome's Observation Tower. Firs within fire hose length were offered protection. Only the summit of Clingmans Dome and Balsam Mountain Road had vehicular access. Mount Le Conte, Mount Guyot, Mount Sterling and other remote fir forests and those firs beyond the reach of a nozzle's spray had to defend themselves.

Crews scouted Fraser firs on Clingmans Dome for signs of adelgid infestation. Magnification through a hand lens was often necessary to spot the insect. Either an ill-looking tree, with a bent "fiddle head–shaped" crown and discolored needles, or the protective, white-woolly mass secreted by the adult were often the first signs of an invasion. By that time, severe damage may have already occurred. Although staff worked aggressively to prevent adelgids from overtaking the highest mountain in the Smokies, the aliens were formidable opponents. Management strategies delayed but could not prevent the persistent progress of the pest.

The BWA, which has challenged scholarly minds, burdened research and management budgets and destroyed acres of Fraser firs, has a fascinating life history. Every single adelgid in this country is female and can reproduce without a male. All of its one hundred to two hundred eggs will hatch as daughters that possess the same potential.

Male adelgids remain in central Europe. European BWAs alternate between fir and spruce trees. Both types of host trees must be available for sexual reproduction. The tree that male adelgids require is not available here, so males remain close to their European homes. Unfortunately for Fraser firs, the female does just fine without him.

The BWAs of the high Smokies nestle in fir bark and hibernate all winter as immature nymphs. None of the other three stages of an adelgid's life can withstand the elements. Covered with a waxy film, its black, tent-shaped body is streaked with a fine, white-hairy mohawk and encircled by a white, waxy fringe to prevent freezing. From March to April, spring finds the female adelgid awake and beginning to mature into an adult.

About the time fir buds begin to break, it becomes a plump, purplish-black, oval body about one millimeter wide, no bigger than the width of a credit card. By June, the mother adelgid will lay around one hundred amber eggs over the next six weeks, securing them to the fir's bark with a waxy thread. For protection, it conceals its body and the eggs in a white, "woolly" mass. Fertilization is not required.

Within a month, or just a few days in warmer weather, red-eyed daughters hatch into orange bodies about one-third of the size of mother. Short legs, but no wings, allow them to move. Relocation is their primary function. If a bird's flight or puff of wind doesn't send the adelgid airborne many miles away, it may be marooned on the same fir tree on which it was born.

Fate dictates its purpose. Find a place to eat. Settle down. Set up camp. Once the "crawler" has selected the perfect spot, it vegetates. It will never see another fir crack, needle, bud or branch again. Unlike an aphid, that can constantly feed and wander around to greener pastures, the adelgid's camp is permanent. Crawlers are the most vulnerable adelgid life stage to insecticidal soaps.

Once it molts, inserts its 1.5-millimeter feeding tube into the bark and injects a hormone to enhance the siphon, sucking will begin after two to eight weeks of rest. This is home. It's the last chip of bark the adelgid will ever know. Its life cycle will be completed here, as a tiny dot, until it dies.

For about a month, the nymph feeds and eventually molts into an adult. Most first-generation adults appear in July in the Smokies. Eggs are laid, and the life cycle is completed. To complete the cycle, adelgids go from egg to crawler to nymph to adult; two to three generations can occur each year, depending on the weather. The Smokies' second-generation adults are usually seen mid-September.

Think about it. Up to fifty thousand reproductive, female adelgids can occupy one Fraser fir. Each female can lay over one hundred eggs. Each of its one hundred daughters can lay another one hundred that year, and each

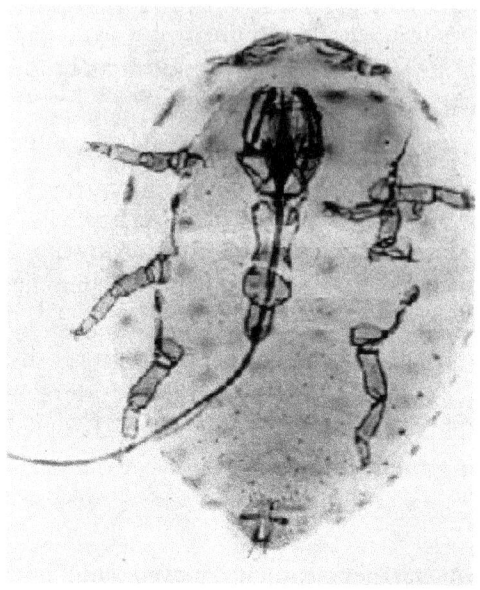

Microscopic view of balsam woolly adelgid. *Courtesy of NPS.*

of its granddaughters can… Thank heavens for Clingmans' cold winters. By late fall, only the settled nymphs will survive the freezing weather.

Knowing the numbers is crucial. No one knows their value more than Kristine Johnson. Monitoring the survival and reproductive success of BWAs, and their impact on the ecosystem, has been a priority for GSMNP staff for decades.

Estimates of BWAs on Clingmans Dome, Mount Le Conte, Mount Sterling and Balsam Mountain are taken annually. Adelgids are inspected within a one-hundred-centimeter grid on Fraser bark. In 2011, the numbers were promising. For the first time in the park's history since the BWA invasion, no adelgids were counted on Mount Le Conte. The fewest numbers annually counted since 1986 were documented on Clingmans Dome, Mount Sterling and Balsam Mountain.

Impact studies are conducted every ten years. Since 1990, the national park has worked jointly with researchers at University of Tennessee–Knoxville to monitor the effects that BWAs have had on the environment. On five summits, sixty-six- by sixty-six-foot designated plots are studied in thirty-six different areas of GSMNP. Fir seedling regeneration is noted. Have some mature firs survived the invasion? Opportunistic plants, now finding open, unshaded space, are identified.

The current news is encouraging. Not only are there fewer adelgids, but females are also laying fewer eggs. One-hundred-egg clutches were initially noted in white woolly masses. Now, twenty eggs per female is the norm.

What challenges will the next generation of Fraser firs bring? Few mature firs remain. But Fraser firs produce many seeds. Numerous second-generation saplings are coming of age. Although adelgid numbers are diminished, are there enough left to rebound, clone themselves and repopulate the new generation of firs? Will BWA numbers increase now that they have a fresh,

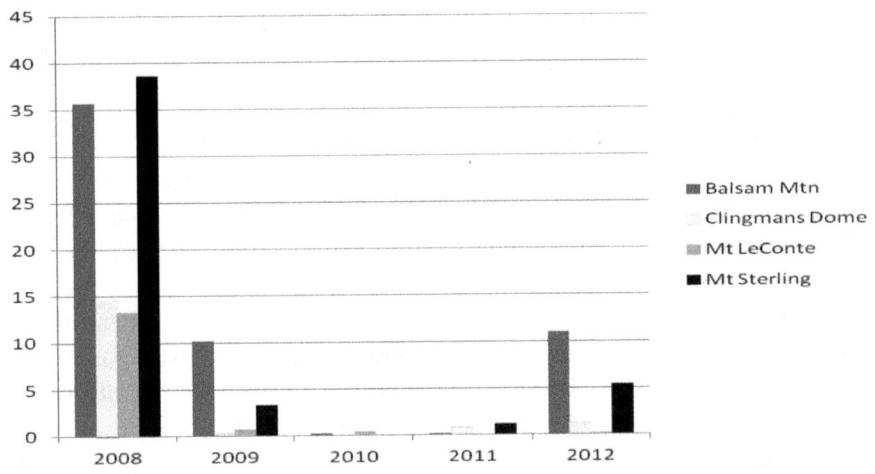

Balsam woolly adelgid 2012 status graph. *Courtesy of Glenn Taylor, GSMNP.*

new, healthy forest to invade? What happens as the new fir generation begins to mature? Will there just be another cycle of infestation?

Or has nature and evolution allowed second-generation Fraser firs to develop a means of resistance that their ancestors did not possess? Will their bark be thicker, more difficult for BWAs to penetrate? What changes in the environment—air and water quality, global warming, soil chemistry—will add cumulative effects? Will the next generation of firs need our help? Will we have the resources to intervene?

Fir forests on Mount Guyot and Mount Sterling that were affected twenty years earlier than those on Clingmans Dome are showing healthy signs of fir regeneration. Other high-elevation sites, though, have been consumed by brambles. Chief Forester Kristine Johnson, NPS staff and researchers remain diligent. Scientific study and monitoring continue.

A tantalizing mystery may hold secrets that will protect the Fraser fir's future. Small stands of large, ancient firs exist. One group thrives on Mount Buckley, one-half mile southwest of Clingmans Dome. Another is on Mount Love, one half mile northeast. These remnants have intrigued scientists. In the middle of acres of massive destruction, these regal trees have survived, relatively unaffected by the uninvited guest. How have they remained immune?

Most scientists agree: developing resistance to the BWA is the key to saving Fraser firs. Identifying resistant trees in their natural settings is underway.

Curiously, firs on Mount Rogers in Virginia have shown greater resistance to the BWA than other fir forests in the Southern Appalachians. Genetic studies are being conducted to determine why. Some advocate transplanting Mount Rogers' resistant trees into infested areas.

Graft cuttings of resistant trees may allow scientists to genetically breed resistant firs. Reintroduced into natural stands, these trees may help control adelgid destruction. Understanding the European silver fir, the adelgid's host tree in its native land, may offer answers. Thousands of BWAs may feed on a silver fir, but the tree remains healthy. The silver fir responds differently to the insect than the Fraser fir does. Silver firs protect themselves. No dense, woody wall is formed around the penetrating stylet. Instead, the silver fir's woody cells die around the injury, limiting the adelgid's food supply.

Bark sampling is another method of scientific study. Studying the fir's bark allows researchers to determine the host's response to the insect, to identify any evidence of resistance and to locate juvabione, a hormone that may interfere with the insect's reproduction. Researchers at North Carolina State University (NCSU) are taking a look at a tree's resistance from a molecular level. Microarray analysis may offer a genetic solution to remedy the fir's response to BWAs and the tree's ability to defend itself.

NCSU is not only interested in preserving native firs but also in developing options to protect Fraser firs grown on Christmas tree plantations. With its resinous odor, stiff branches, triangular shape, dark green color, long needle life and rounded base, the Fraser fir has become a popular Christmas tree. Almost twenty-five thousand acres of farms in North Carolina raise over fifty million Fraser firs, generating a hefty economic boost for the region. Fir farms use pesticides, predatory beetles and other measures to control BWA.

Scientists recognize the value in continued research for both fir plantations and protected national parklands. A whole community depends on their survival in native forests. Several mosses, liverworts and plant species live only in spruce-fir forests. Some insects and amphibians do too. High-elevation songbirds return to breed in their canopies. Partners in Flight, a bird conservation group, joins other organizations to monitor changes in bird populations in all types of forest habitats. Their "Southern Blue Ridge Bird Conservation Plan" (1999) states: "The extensive deterioration of this ecosystem (red spruce-Fraser fir forests) now garners the most attention from conservationists."

GSMNP managers have had their sights on the future. Select firs found at different altitudes, growing in six separate fir forests in the park, are protected. Preserving a diverse gene pool of original fir-tree stock was imperative. If the pest couldn't be removed from the forest, national park officials decided, a plan to protect and preserve the future of forest specimens until BWAs were controlled should be implemented.

In 1995, GSMNP was deeded Purchase Knob, an old family homesite and Christmas tree plantation adjacent to the park. Seeds were collected from thirteen sites (including Waterrock Knob on the Blue Ridge Parkway) to produce six hundred Fraser fir seedlings, planted in a protected area on Purchase Knob. Perhaps scientific study there will provide an effective management option for the balsam woolly adelgid. Perhaps effective means to control the hemlock woolly adelgid, discovered in the park in 2002 destroying its 1,500 acres of hemlocks *(Tsuga canadensis)*, will be effective in controlling both pests. Or, just maybe, nature will provide the solutions without us.

Often, the Fraser fir is chosen as the national Christmas tree for the White House. No finer fir specimen could symbolize a country's regal, stately pride. But to save the Fraser fir is not for beauty alone. The Fraser fir presides over its forest like a leader over his country. A whole ecosystem depends on it.

CHAPTER 6

FINDING A FLOWER OR TWO

Life at the top is tough. Plants must adapt to extreme conditions to live there. Short growing seasons, strong winds, bitter cold temperatures and shallow soils all contribute to their challenges. To fulfill their purpose in life—to bloom, attract, connect, make seed and reproduce—plants in the high Smokies have developed special traits. Stiff stems, leathery leaves and ground-hugging habits help them survive. Some accept more shade than sun. Others bloom three weeks later than valley relatives, waiting for spring's warm rays to find them up high.

Fewer types of flora live at higher elevations, but some rarities are rooted there. One wildflower grows nowhere else in the world. Some prefer the cool, shady climates. Others descend from plants deserted here after the last glacial period. Canada should be their home, not the Southern Appalachians.

In May, find a few members of the heath family blooming on Clingmans Dome. Heath plants, typically with bell-shaped flowers and evergreen leaves, usually grow in acidic soils. The rounded, five-foot-tall highbush blueberry (*Vaccinium corymbosum*) produces greenish-white blooms. Juicy dark-blue berries provide wildlife with delicious fruit by fall. If a late spring frost kills tender buds, fall fruit production is scarce. Animals preparing for winter suffer.

Dog hobble (*Leucothoe fontanesiana*) will snare the hound to save the bear. Sprawling, weak branches rest on neighbors, forming thickets three to five feet tall. So dense are the tangles, some say they could snag bear dogs chasing their prey. Its scientific name, however, honors a beautiful Persian princess. White, urn-shaped flower clusters dangle from arched branches.

CLINGMANS DOME

Between Newfound Gap and Clingmans Dome. Hoarfrost on wild parsnip or Queen Anne's lace. February 11, 1940. *Courtesy of Albert "Dutch" Roth Collection, University of Tennessee–Knoxville Libraries.*

Plant witch hobble (*Viburnum lantanoides*), also known as hobblebush or mosewood, beside your front door, and witches, be gone! Or just look for mass colonies along the Spruce-Fir Nature Trail and the paved Dome trail. Long, irregular branches park large round leaves opposite one another. Flowers resemble hydrangeas. Outer, wide, sterile flowers attract pollinators to the small fertile ones in the center. Forest creatures dine on bright red berries in August. A palette full of paint splatters the leaves in early fall, turning an otherwise monotonous, evergreen fir forest to brilliant life. In some locations, leaves turn a wonderful bronze color. New Englanders call it moosewood. A large northern mammal enjoys its woody bark.

A high-elevation relative is red elderberry (*Sambucus racemosa ssp.pubens*), a cousin to the lowlander: black or common elderberry (*S. canadensis*). Make sweet wine or jelly from the black berries of the lowlander, but the scarlet, nonpoisonous berries of red elderberry in August are bitter and inedible. Flat-topped flower heads form fruits on the black elderberry. A pinkish-cream, cone-shaped flower cluster adorns the red. See red elderberry in moist soils along Clingmans Dome Road.

Look in May, along the parking area, for rose family members in bloom. But look up, not down. Related in structure to garden roses, these roses

In November 2011, a female bear was hit by a car on Newfound Gap Road. University of Tennessee–Knoxville's veterinarian evaluated the compound fracture of her right hind leg. Surgery was a major risk. Two options remained: 1) euthanize her, or 2) let Nature take care of her. After antibiotics and a day's rest, she was released far from the highway, near her former territory. A radio-collar allowed the NPS to check on her in mid-winter. When Joe Yarkovich, NPS wildlife biologist, followed radio signals to her den in February 2012, he found her wounds healed and three healthy cubs. *Photo courtesy of Joe Yarkovich.*

Left: NPS spraying for balsam woolly adelgids on Clingmans Dome. *Courtesy of Glenn Taylor, GSMNP biologist.*

Below: Mushrooms beside the Appalachian Trail on Mount Buckley, 2012. *Photo by the author.*

Bumblebees competing for pink turtlehead nectar near Clingmans Dome Tower. *Photo by Brooke Lyda.*

Thunderhead sandstone with concretions. *Photo by Bill Lea.*

A healthy Fraser fir branch with female cones upright, purple with pale-green bracts on the A.T. between Clingmans Dome and Mount Buckley. *Photo by the author.*

Above: A three-year-old Fraser fir seedling was infested with balsam woolly adelgids in a lab at the Department of Entomology at North Carolina State University. Eighteen months later, the results were graphic. *Courtesy of Leslie Newton.*

Left: Carolina Northern Flying Squirrel. *Photo by Mike LaVoie; provided by NCWRC.*

Magnified Michaux's saxifrage. *Courtesy of Scott Dean, field botanist/educator.*

Painted trillium. *Courtesy of Scott Dean, field botanist/educator.*

Purple-fringed orchid on the Forney Ridge Trail. *Photo by Christi Worsham.*

A black bear may stand on its hind legs, not in aggression, but to see greater distances. *Photo by Bill Lea.*

Spruce-fir moss spider (magnified). *Courtesy of Glenn Taylor, GSMNP biologist.*

Rarely seen bobcats inhabit Clingmans Dome. *Photo by Bill Lea.*

This view from the Dome parking lot shows fall colors in the valley and rime ice at high elevation. *Photo by Bill Lea.*

Coyotes roam all park elevations. *Photo by Bill Lea.*

American black bear (*Ursus americanus*). *Photo by Bill Lea.*

Ruffed grouse forage along Clingmans Dome Road. *Photo by Bill Lea.*

Bear eating mountain ash berries. *Photo by Bill Lea.*

Aerial view of Clingmans Dome. *Courtesy of Bill Vinson, Red Chair Architects.*

Clingmans Dome Tower, 2012. *Photo by author.*

Above: View from Clingmans Dome. *Photo by Bill Lea.*

Left: Rugel's Indian plantain. *Photo by Christi Worsham.*

Above: Red-cheeked salamander, Spruce-fir Nature Trail. *Photo by the author.*

Left: On the Appalachian Trail, crossing the Dome. *Photo by the author.*

are trees. Botanical family members have similar flower structures. Roses have five petals, many stamens and a cup at the base of each flower. Part of a huge extended family, roses can be garden shrubs, brambles, flowers or fruit trees.

The American mountain ash tree (*Sorbus americana*) is a rose, not an ash. It should be in Canada, not south at Clingmans Dome. No greater botanical beauty exists in the high Smokies in September. Some years, compact clusters of white flowers in May, like those of the black elderberry, turn to showy, bright orange-red berries in the fall. Massive red mounds drape along forest-green, compound leaves. Handfuls of holly berries come to mind. But inspect closer. Each berry looks like a tiny, individual apple. A five-pointed star forms on the bottom. Sliced in half, the berry's interior resembles the fleshy chambers of an apple, also a member of the rose family.

During those fall years of massive production, bears may be seen in the thin branches, consuming paw-fulls of berries as winter approaches. Mountain ash fruits are very sour but, like apples, become sweeter after a good frost.

Blackberry bushes are roses, too. Thornless blackberries (*Rubus canadensis*) grow in giant groves along the Dome trail. Like the red elderberry, mountain ash and others, blackberries have filled sun-drenched hillsides left open by dying Fraser fir. As aggressive competitors, the blackberries' arching canes can grow up to eight feet in their first year. The second year, they'll flower, fruit and die. Brown, woody skeletons remain for another year, and then new sprouts emerge. Birds eat the juicy berries, passing undigested seeds across wide areas. Brambles can overcome hillsides, crowding out shorter, smaller wildflowers also seeking the sun.

Another rose is a cherry, the pin cherry. Very few hardwood trees join evergreens high on mountain ridges where winters are long and cold. But the deciduous pin cherry (*Prunus pensylvanica*), the mountain ash and the yellow birch (*Betula alleghaniensis*) do. All three withstand bitter elements by establishing rootholds in disturbed open areas. Known to readily repopulate an area after a fire, the pin cherry has also been called the fire cherry. In May or June, look for clusters of white flowers just as its new, slender leaves appear. Small, shiny red fruits form in August, providing more soft mast for hungry wildlife. Although the pin cherry is usually a small, short-lived tree, a champion, seventy-five feet tall, grows in the Smokies.

Several low-growing wildflowers near Clingmans Dome also bloom May to June. Nine species of trilliums are found in the Smokies; two prefer shady, moist, forest floors at higher elevations. The painted trillium (*Trillium undulatum*) is the loveliest of all. Its wavy, soft edges and pink-streaked white petals make it unique among trilliums. The bright pink "V" at the base of each petal appears to have been painted by the delicate, loving hand of an artist. As with all trilliums, related to the lily family, three flower petals rest above three green sepals and are attached to a stem of three whorled leaves.

Tucked among galax and rhododendron, find the ripe, red fall berries of the painted trillium in August. Ants may have gotten there first. Worldwide, ants are known to disperse seeds of over three thousand plant species. Trilliums are particularly alluring. Attached to the seed is a fatty structure that ants find hard to resist. Back at their underground colony, the tasty substance is consumed. The discarded seed becomes "planted" somewhere in the refuse pile of an anthill. Beetles, slugs and yellow jackets are also attracted to trillium seeds, but their dispersal distance is more limited.

Stinking Benjamin also lives up high. Known, too, as the erect trillium or wake robin (*Trillium erectum*), its petals are deep maroon; at lower elevations in the park, they're white. Three features make it unique: the dark-colored, rather than yellow, center; its flower perched boldly erect above its broad whorled leaves; and its foul odor, similar to that of a wet dog. Like all trilliums, it takes six years for it to bloom. By fall, juicy dark red berries hold dozens of seeds.

Some lily family members arrive early. Canada mayflower (*Maianthemum canadense*) is a rebel lily. Instead of the standard three or six parts to a lily flower, this species grows flower parts in twos or fours. Standing only two to eight inches tall, it spreads by underground stems forming large colonies. Carpeting conifer forest floors near Andrews Bald and along the Appalachian Trail between Clingmans Dome and Newfound Gap, its small fragrant white flowers dust the landscape like a light snowfall. Two heart-shaped glossy leaves clasp the stem, almost encircling it. The short stem zigzags its way upward, as if resisting the tight hug. Flowers fade into brown-spotted berries that turn a deep red lasting throughout the winter.

The rose twisted stalk (*Streptopus roseus*) also has a zigzag stem. It, too, can be seen under spruces along the Appalachian Trail near Indian Gap. Rosy, bell-shaped flowers dangle from leaf joints. Each petal curves backward with age. Alternating leaves parade up jointed, arching stems forming two distinct rows. With greater scrutiny, one sees dark red streaks on each blossom and fine, short hairs edging each leaf. Deep parallel leaf veins help identify it as a lily family member. Late summer, cherry-red berries mature.

Along Clingmans Dome Road and the Spruce-Fir Nature Trail, bluebead or Clinton's lily (*Clintonia borealis*) opens loose clusters of creamy-yellow, nodding flowers in May. An impressive group grows near a shady rock outcrop on Mount Buckley. Flowers top a ten-inch stalk rising above three basal, leathery leaves. Berries are porcelain blue. Its low-altitude cousin, speckled wood lily or white Clintonia (*C. umbellulata*) has white flowers with purple dots; berries are black. Clintonia is named for naturalist and New York governor DeWitt Clinton.

Look down—way down. Watch your step along the Spruce-Fir Nature Trail. The ground-hugging, feminine mountain wood sorrel (*Oxalis montana*) blooms June to July in the cool, moist shade. Dainty, clover-like leaves, notched at the tips, are divided into threes. Five-petaled flowers, faintly streaked with thin, pink veins, close at night. Look for the yellow-dotted accent at the base of each petal. Look also for the closed flower beneath the whorl of leaves. It produces its own seed. If an insect pollinator fails to fertilize the open one, the sorrel has a second chance. Creeping rhizomes and explosive seed capsules spread huge sorrel beds over the mossy floor. Of the five sorrels that grow in the park, this one prefers high mountains. All oxalis leaves, though, provide a lemony, acid taste to salads.

Yellow trout lily or yellow adder's tongue (*Erythronium americanum*) is common in high, moist fir forests as well as lower elevations. Six identical yellow petals and sepals roll backward, exposing long brown or yellow anthers. A single flower head towers above a pair of trout-patterned, greenish-brown leaves at the base. Thick underground stems form large, expanding trout lily communities. Deer love them. Through its roots to their leaves, trout lilies siphon up phosphorus, a valuable element in a deer's diet. Like the trillium, this wildflower is slow to mature, taking over seven years to bloom.

One lily blooms later in the season. Turk's cap lily *(Lilium superbum)*, the tallest lily in eastern America, blooms in profusion near Clingmans Dome Parking Lot during late summer. Find it also along the A.T. between the Dome and Mount Buckley. Over a dozen brilliant orange flowers, with six matching, deeply inverted petals and sepals, nod their heads atop six- to eight-foot-tall flower stalks. Purple dots splatter upper surfaces. A central green star, with a yellow center, directs pollinators to the nectary. Whorled leaves span out like opened umbrellas along the tall stout stem. Frequent winds through the gap, swinging the yellowish-orange banners like flags on a ship, make a photographic capture challenging, but it is well worth the effort. Native Americans used to harvest the scaly underground bulb for food.

Twenty-three thousand orchids, the largest flower family in the world, live mostly in the tropics. A rare spectacular orchid beauty, however, tucks itself between bushy vegetation on the south side of the paved trail to the tower.

Other small purple-fringed orchids (*Platanthera psycodes*)—a magnificent, fragrant showstopper—are found along Clingmans Dome Road and Forney Ridge Trail. From June to July, numerous lilac flowers cluster at the top of a one-foot-tall stem. The lower lip, a three-lobed, deeply fringed petal, attracts pollinators like a landing strip at an airport. Fringes, heavily loaded with pollen, dust the backs of insects as they reach for nectar deep in the flower spur. The species name, *psycodes*, means "butterfly," with the frilly lower lip resembling a dainty butterfly alighting to investigate.

The large purple-fringed orchid (*P. grandiflora*) also grows at higher elevations in the Smokies. The flower cluster is larger and wider. A hand lens may be helpful to see the round tubular opening leading to the nectary at the base of the petals. The small purple-fringed orchid has a bow-tie shaped opening.

Nodding ladies' tresses (*Spiranthes cernua*), also orchids, thrive on moist banks of high ridges. Flowering August through November, it is one of the latest-blooming orchids in the park. Look for colonies on the Forney Ridge Trail toward Andrews Bald. Magnify the twisted flower stalk to see knobby hairs along its stem and tiny, pure white tubular flowers.

It's hard to mistake a mint. Square stems, opposite leaves, two-lipped flowers (with two lobes up, three lobes down) and four stamens (one pair long, the other, short) all reveal the family characteristics of Clingman's hedge-nettle *(Stachys clingmanii)*. Named by John K. Small for Clingmans Dome, this species only grows in the Southern Appalachians. From July to August, look for its knee-high, pale purple flower clusters blooming along the trail to the tower. Also, look beside the base of the tower's ramp. Dense hairs protrude from stem angles but are absent on flat surfaces. Only long-tongued insects can successfully pollinate the deep throat.

Follow hummingbirds, swallowtail butterflies and bumblebees to the most gorgeous member of the mints. It's absolutely impossible to miss crimson bee balm or Oswego tea (*Monarda didyma*). From July to September, brilliant, cardinal-red crowns of bee balm reign three to six feet over lower vegetation in massive gardens along Clingmans Dome Road, parking lot and trail. The round flower cluster is composed of individual flower heads of two-lipped petals. The three-lobed, ragged lower lip is longer than the thin, erect upper one. Tufts of hair at the ends of the lower lobes make them appear even longer. Two long, pollen-coated stamens protrude from each flower. Bees love the tasty nectar, but hummingbirds can penetrate the long tube more efficiently.

Young leaves and petals will season salads and fried potatoes. Bee balm makes a nice minty tea; steeped leaves relieve indigestion. In the British

A hedge-nettle on Clingmans Dome Trail, July 2012. *Photo by the author.*

rebellion, American settlers dumped gallons of tea in the Boston Harbor. Native Oswego Indians offered this mint tea as a substitute.

Step into the forest. On the A.T., across the road from the Spruce-Fir Nature Trail, find a unique flower—one that only grows in GSMNP and nowhere else on the planet. Showy, it is not, but special, it truly is. Rugel's Indian plantain (*Rugelia nudicaulis*) is a member of the aster or sunflower family. Pale yellowish-brown disks form, but rays do not.

Crimson bee balm on Clingmans Dome Road, July 2012. *Photo by the author.*

Take a relative, like the daisy, and pluck the "He-loves-me; He-loves-me-not" rays from the edge. Fade the remaining disk from a bright to dull yellow. Sprinkle in some long, straggly, brown stigmas, split them partially in half and twist them in opposite directions. Squeeze the disk to the size of your thumbnail. Imagine several of these nodding from the top of a foot-tall stem. Now, you have a Rugel's.

Better yet, leave the Dome parking lot and find a healthy colony midway along the Clingmans Dome Bypass Trail. Or head south 1.5 miles from Clingmans Dome to Mount Buckley. Among ferns and mosses, beside the trail, is a Rugel colony. They raise their heads from July to August. The Rugel is rare, indeed, but in its personal space, it grows abundantly.

Rugel's should grow on Mount Buckley. Rugel's Indian plantain is named for the botanist who discovered it, Ferdinand Rugel. Mr. Rugel made numerous botanical excursions with his friend Samuel Buckley, the geologist/botanist who joined Senator Clingman on his 1858 expedition.

Take your trekking pole. Gently push aside a frond-to-frond covering of ferns along Goshen Prong trail near the Dome. Rugel colonies hide there. The beauty that nature deprived in bud is compensated in leaf. A cluster of four-inch-long, toothed leaves encircle each stem. Detailed vein arrangements imprint each heart-shaped leaf as if embroidered by a seamstress. Did nature borrow that design from violets? Let no one claim Rugel's is unattractive. Observe the whole package. For further proof, see the colony at the Forney Creek and Forney Ridge Trail juncture.

Rugel's family name, aster, is Latin for "star," describing the flower head. The world's second-largest flowering family, the aster claims twenty to thirty members in GSMNP. Asters seem to have one large flower head—not so. Like a good botanist, inspect closer. Remember the familiar daisy? The yellow center is actually dozens (even thousands!) of itty-bitty, individual flowers crowded together, each producing its own teeny-tiny seed. White "He-loves-me-not," petal-like rays surround the central disk. Ray flowers are often sterile and don't form seeds. Their primary function is to attract pollinators.

Aster seeds feed many fall and winter songbirds. Pearl crescent, silvery checkerspot and some fritallary butterflies lay their eggs on asters. Caterpillars hatch, feed on their host plants, rest, spin a chrysalis and then pupate, waiting for a change. Identifying an aster species can be tricky. Ray flowers come in different colors. Disks vary, too. Yellow disks may turn red or purple with age. Consider the entire plant. Look at leaves, stem and flower. Note its habitat. Is it dry or wet? What's the elevation?

No, those aren't golden black-eyed Susans (*Rudbeckia hirta*) gathering among red bee balms along the Dome trail from August to September. Look at their "eyes." Cutleaf coneflowers (*R. laciniata*) have green "eyes" that lengthen with age. Narrow ray flowers gently droop. Deeply cut lower leaves should be watched. Biologists look for purplish-brown spots, which could be an indicator of poor health caused by air pollution.

A few asters grow only at higher elevations. Seen along Clingmans Dome Road late summer and early fall, the mountain wood aster (*Eurybia chlorolepis*) has a daisy-like head, with ten or more rays. Its similar cousin at lower elevations, white wood aster (*Eurybia divaricata*), has fewer than ten rays per head.

The whorled wood aster (*Oclemena acuminata*) is a faker—it's not whorled at all. The tightly arranged alternate leaf pattern only creates that illusion. Did the one who named this aster get fooled, or was he testing our scientific observation skills? One of the earliest asters to bloom, the "whorled" aster is common along Clingmans Dome Road July though October. Underground runners create huge beds. A yellow or red disk is surrounded by ten to seventeen white rays.

Look for another aster growing along the Dome road and tower trail. Large cottony beds are encircled by the tower ramp. Like Rugel's, the rays are absent. Only clustered, pure-white disk flowers appear. Protruding white stigmas create a soft, feathery appearance. White snakeroot (*Ageratina altissima*), one of thirteen snakeroots in the park, is common in the Southern Appalachians, but some consider it a weed. From July to September, dense colonies of four-foot-tall branching stalks balance small flower heads in broad, flat-topped clusters. Seeds attached to fuzzy white tails are dispersed by the wind.

Native Americans used white snakeroot to treat snakebites. However, the plant is highly poisonous. Cattle grazing on the plant can ingest the toxin, transferring it to their milk. Humans drinking large quantities of tainted milk could develop milk sickness. Reportedly, Abraham Lincoln's mother died from this disorder in 1818. Dr. Anna Pierce Bixby linked the disease to snakeroot in the 1830s, and pioneers became more cautious.

Ancient Greeks used asters for snakebites. A poultice was also created by beating plant parts with hog grease and was applied to the bite of a "mad dog." Dried goldenrods, another aster, stopped bleeding from wartime wounds. Goldenrod seeds could thicken a stew; dried flowers made a nice tea.

Skunk goldenrod (*Solidago glomerata*) is endemic to only thirteen counties of Tennessee and North Carolina. Fields and pastures make perfect habitats for most goldenrods, but not the skunk. Grassy balds, spruce-fir forests and high rocky ridges attract this rare species. See it along the Dome trail. From August to October, about ten golden, ray flowers encircle fifteen golden disk flowers. Most goldenrods produce curved, one-sided clusters of tiny flowers. The skunk, however, ends in a large yellow bouquet. Note its large basal leaves. Take a whiff. The unpleasant odor does not come from its flowers nor its crushed leaves. It's thought to be a sulfur mist surrounding the plant from decomposing vegetation. Flowers fade, seeds take flight and stalks die with the first frost; new green growth will shoot from the root come spring.

Traditional Uses of High-elevation Plant Species

by Ila Hatter, interpreter-naturalist for Great Smoky Mountain Institute and others, author of Edibles and Medicinals of Southern Appalachia *and host of UNC-TV (PBS) "Folkways" programs.*

Filmy Angelica (*Angelica triquinata*)
Cherokee families once climbed the high mountains to collect their "Jellico Greens" in the spring. As there are toxic relatives and look-alikes to this plant, one must be absolutely sure of the identification. But it was so well known by the Cherokee that there is even a "Jellico Mountain" in Tennessee.

Bee Balm, Oswego Tea (*Monarda didyma*)
Though tea from the dried leaves and flowers was a common remedy among mountain-folk for coughs and colds, it is not "minty" in flavor. It contains the same active ingredient in mouthwash: thymol, which is what makes it a good antiseptic. (The tea from fresh leaves will taste like Listerine!)

Blueberry (*Vaccinium corymbosum*)
In some high elevations the mountain families found such abundance of blueberries that many jars were canned for winter storage. One family boasted of "100 jars" put by. "Blueberry Dumplings" were simply made by cooking the berries with honey in a cast-iron stew pot and dropping biscuit dough into the bubbling berries until "cooked through and purple-blue." Blackberries could also be served in this manner. The leaves of blueberry species were a traditional medicine tea to reduce "high sugar" (diabetes).

Clingman's Hedge-Nettle (*Stachys clingmanii*)
Though a member of the mint family, it carries no familiar fragrance. Some sources call it "rank-smelling." Commonest traditional use was the leaves applied as a healing poultice

or to staunch bleeding wounds. Some "wound-worts" have abundant underground tubers eaten raw, boiled, baked or pickled.

Cut-Leaved Coneflower (*Rudbeckia laciniata*)
The popular "Sochan" of the Cherokee. Usually found near water or damp places and in valleys, many still say the most flavorful grow on high mountain slopes. The greens are gathered in spring when only one to two feet high. They can be par-boiled and then fried in a skillet with "fat-back" or bacon. There are fundraising "Indian Dinners" in Cherokee, North Carolina, where Sochan greens are served with fried trout, bean bread and ramps (wild leeks).

Michaux's Saxifrage (*Saxafraga michauxii*)
Found growing in "seeps" or directly in streams or waterfalls, the common name is "Brook Lettuce." Young leaves taste like lettuce and are served as a "kilt-salad" in "mountain-talk." A hot dressing of vinegar, sugar and bacon is poured over the fresh "lettuce," which wilts or "kills" the greens. Sliced onions or ramps are an optional addition.

Mountain Ash, Rowan (*Sorbus americana*)
"Their spells were vain. The Hags returned
To their queen in sorrowful mood,
Crying that witches have no power
Where thrives the Rowan-tree wood."

For centuries, Europeans revered the rowan tree for its protective powers. Branches were often used for dowsing rods and magic wands. Two twigs tied together with red thread in a cross was carried as a protective amulet against sorcery or placed over a doorway. Walking sticks made of rowan wood were thought to protect man and beast from unseen terrors as they roamed. The British are familiar still today with rowanberry bitters, rowanberry wine and a tart jelly made from the orange-red berries. It is made in combination with wild crabapples and typically served with meat dishes, especially venison.

Are you depressed? Either medicinally or aesthetically, the mountain St. John's wort (*Hypericum graveolens*) can lift your spirits, or perhaps its aroma can. It's not offensive like the skunk goldenrod but enticing—the essence of sweet butterscotch. Centuries ago, priests used St. John's wort to avert evil spirits and illness. The term "wort" previously meant "root" but later meant "those plants with healing properties." "St. John" refers to St. John the Baptist Festival Day, June 24, the longest day of summer when bright flowers bloom.

Mountain St. John's wort, beside the Dome Trail, is also a native specialty, growing only in the high Southern Appalachians. Over a foot tall, the golden yellow, five-petaled flowers from July to September beckon one closer. Ten long, thin stamens project from its golden center, creating a starburst effect. Simple, opposite leaves are splattered with dark glands or black dots. A pigment from these dots, called hypercin (hence, its scientific name), is the substance used as an antidepressant.

Scan cliffs from the Dome Parking Lot in July. Groundwater seeps down rocky surfaces in a perpetual trickle. No better environment is suitable for Michaux's saxifrage (*Saxifraga michauxii*). Pull out your hand lens; you'll need a botanist's eye to appreciate its magnificent design. The delicate white flower, under magnification, reveals secrets that differentiate this species from other members of its family. Five tiny, white petals form. Three stalked, upper spade-like petals are larger than the spoon-like, bottom two. Pairs of yellow, glandular dots accent the base of each large petal but are absent on the smaller ones. Reddish-orange knobs tip the ends of ten stamens for a nice contrast.

A widely branched, hairy stem holds the flowers above a basal rosette of deeply toothed leaves. Older leaves have turned burgundy. Mats of Michaux seem to grow straight out of the rocks. "Saxifrage" in Latin means "to break rock." Neither is true, of course. Harsh high-elevation winters freeze and thaw the moist cliffs in repeated cycles. Rock surfaces chip and crack over time; organic matter fills the void, and the tenacious Michaux's roots cling tight. A glacial relic, Michaux's saxifrage can only be found in the Southeast.

Filmy angelica (*Angelica triquinata*) commands attention in August and September. Along the Dome Road and Tower Trail, angelica rules. Four-inch-wide, flat-topped clusters of tiny, greenish-yellow flowers are held atop three- to six-foot-tall celery-like stalks. Like little saucers, these flower heads offer pollinators their sweet candy. Bees become so addicted that they're reluctant to leave. Often, they sip to excess. No longer sober, bees stumble, roll and may fall off the table.

Botanists call this flower design an "umbel." Take an upside-down approach. Short ribs of an opened umbrella come into view. Characteristic of the parsley family, the angelica has multiple layers of umbrellas. Flower stems radiate from the top of the stalk. At the tip of those stems, more umbrellas open. All parsleys have hollow tubes. Many family members are familiar spices: cumin, coriander, dill and fennel. Some have edible roots, like carrots. Filmy angelica, some say, is highly poisonous.

Purple stalks have a hazy or "filmy" coating. A large, filmy sheath partially wraps the base of the leaves. Legend claims that an angel told a monk about the plant's curative properties. Angelica was thought to repel evil spirits, witches and the plague. History reports that angelica was protected by Michael the Archangel because it bloomed on May 8 (on the Julian calendar), Michael's feast day.

Gentians add color in the fall. Family traits are consistent. Four or five fused petals form tubular flowers. A stamen is attached to each petal, leaves are opposite and a capsule contains many seeds. Two of four gentians in the park prefer high elevations. Stiff gentian (*Gentianella quinquefolia*) is distinctive. As many as fifty small, erect blossoms are seen on one plant. Blooming late August until frost, pale blue or violet lobes come to a point, like miniature sharpened pencils. Bristled tips highlight the effect. Paired leaves clasp the four-angled stem. A bed of stiffs covers the bank behind the exhibit board at the Dome parking lot. More grow within twenty steps down the Forney Ridge trail. Look closely; they're often overlooked.

Slip a snip of gentian in gin. It may be the bitterest herb in the world. Bitters, like artichoke leaves, angelica root, quinine, dandelion and gentian, stimulate the gallbladder to produce bile, aiding in digestion. Bitters also stimulate the appetite. Before hops, gentian was used to brew beer. Today, gentian is still used in a few aperitifs.

The mountain gentian (*Gentiana decora*) is not often seen. Search the A.T. between Clingmans Dome and Silers Bald. Late fall, pale blue, funnel-shaped flowers are larger and fewer in number than the stiff.

It's hard to believe that the monkshood is a buttercup. Like lemony-yellow buttercups dotting an open field, wild monkshood (*Aconitum uncinatum*) is a member of the family. The buttercup family has a long ancestry. Family traits resemble those of plants that lived millions of years ago. Gentians and asters are more advanced, more evolved. They've developed fewer, more specialized flower parts. Generally, modern flowers have one pistil, the female organ that receives pollen to produce seeds. The primitive, simple buttercups, however, have three or more pistils.

Buttercup sepals often match the color of the petals. Wild monkshood has five deep-purple sepals (leaf-like structures). The uppermost sepal forms a helmet-like shelter over a dark purple, two-petaled flower. Like other buttercup relatives, such as columbines, delphiniums and larkspurs, the "simple" monkshood has a complex-looking flower arrangement.

The monkshood needs help. Four-feet-tall, slender, weak stems cannot remain erect. Stems and flowers creep across nearby vegetation. Deeply lobed, coarsely toothed leaves resemble maple leaves. Endemic to the Southern Appalachians, it prefers the open areas of a spruce-fir forest.

Monkshood juices are poisonous. Like Amazon natives indebted to the poison dart frog, Native Americans coated arrow tips with monkshood. Bees love its nectar, though. From August to October, robust bumblebees bully their way into covered nectaries, brush against pollen, fly to the next flower and dust its pistil tip, just as nature planned.

Bumblebees also like pink turtlehead (*Chelone lyonii*). *Chelone* is Greek for "tortoise." A bumblebee pushes open the "turtle's jaws" to enter. Two-lipped, tubular flowers form in rosy pink, spiked clusters at the end of the stalk. A one-inch-long upper lip arches over a flattened, three-lobed lower one. Pinch the corners of the "turtle's mouth." The center, lower lobe is gently raised. Like fuzz on a duckling, yellow hairs bristle from the base. Spread by rhizome and seed, colonies of pink turtlehead have become established at the juncture of Dome Trail and the A.T. It is only native to the high Southeast.

The purple-flowering raspberry (*Rubus odoratus*) isn't picky about pollinators. Open-handed invitations from wide, purple flowers make nectar readily available. Short legs or jointed ones, slender snout or tiny beak, crawl or buzz, flit or stay—it's all the same. Just grab a little pollen before you go, friend. It's all about reproduction, you know.

The purple-flowering raspberry or thimbleberry belongs to the rose family. Its flower resembles a wild rose: five large, single petals; many stamens; and many styles or pistils. A bushy shrub forming dense thickets, it starts blooming in May. Thornless, arching branches, covered with red hairs, continue to bloom sporadically all summer and into fall. Woody stems crack and peel with age.

Thimble-looking, red berries and large purple flowers may be present at the same time. Robins, cedar waxwings and other birds devour the fruits and disperse the seeds. The shrub is a southern specialty. Some say that it only grows below five thousand feet in elevation. However, the purple-flowering raspberry is climbing Clingmans Dome. Across from the Visitor

Center, a thimbleberry thicket is spreading toward the open ridge, soaking in the rays.

Seasonal weather conditions and changing patterns can alter blooming times of trees, shrubs and herbaceous plants. A late spring frost may kill berry blossoms, reducing fall fruit harvests. Erosion is erratic and rainfall unpredictable. Too wet, too dry, heavy snow, thick ice, strong winds, intense sun—all sculpt, redistribute, punish, retard and even destroy some plant specimens each year. Bird and beast will feed and digest, pass waste and replant. Trees die; canopies open. Increased sunlight kills some and entices others. Tough ones are resilient. Some adapt; others don't. What is blooming one year may not be blooming the next.

Explore, observe and return. More treasures bloom near the high ridges of Clingmans Dome. Massive displays of the spectacular Catawba rhododendron (*Rhododendron catawbiense*) border Clingmans Dome Road. The breathtaking flame azaleas (*Rhododendron calendulaceum*) decorate nearby Andrews Bald in June. Shrubs, like gooseberry, myrtle, minniebush and cranberry are other high-elevation species. Can you find them on the Dome?

Start finding other beauties as you descend below to five thousand feet, leaving the spruce-fir forest zone behind. Return to Clingmans Dome some other season to find a flower or two that you hadn't seen. Perhaps it'll be tucked beside a familiar trail, prompting you to ask yourself, "How did I miss that?" Keep looking. Grab a field guide and a hand lens, and make your own discovery. Find a beauty not mentioned here.

CHAPTER 7

DENNING ON THE DOME

A BEAR'S TALE

She'd been on her own now for over two years. A four-year-old black bear shared her mother's home range on Clingmans Dome, but she rarely saw her. Brother had chosen to roam farther afield to find his own territory.

Winter approached. Along the Dome's trail, flattened vegetation, pressed underneath 150 pounds, marked her frequent foraging paths. Chunks clawed from fir stumps were scattered, a sign she'd been searching for grubs. Since late summer, browsing had increased. If fall harvests were plentiful, she may eat twenty thousand calories in twenty-four hours. By late fall, twenty straight hours of feeding could add three pounds a day.

High-elevation forests had less to offer the bear to eat than the rich diversity of life in lower-elevation, hardwood forests. Studies have shown that bears living among spruce and firs may weigh 28 percent less than well-fed ones in the coves below. A deer carcass might provide a meal. But chasing *live* prey required too much energy. A body built with a short back, thick shoulders, heavy fur coat and forelimbs shorter than back limbs wasn't designed for long-distance running. She could sprint at thirty miles per hour but not for long.

Primarily, she's a vegetarian. Massive blackberry patches beside Clingmans Dome Trail, sprawling in open sun under smooth, gray skeletons of Fraser firs, offered tasty calories. Last year, a late-spring freeze killed berry patch blossoms, destroying the fall berry crop. This year, thankfully, brambleberries were abundant for a quick source of natural sugars. Highbush blueberries and low-growing raspberries were favorite alternatives.

By October, Clingmans Dome provided clusters of orange-red mountain ash berries, made sweeter by the first hard frost. Dead Fraser firs had removed cool, shady canopies. Sun-loving, high-elevation mountain ash now covered many slopes.

High in the tree's spindly canopy, front paws pulled draping branches, laden with berries, close to her snout. For hours, she gorged on large quantities, shifting her position within the same tree. With skill and grace, she gulped voraciously. Overindulgence, however, overwhelmed her short digestive system.

Black bears have two-part stomachs. Food passes into a large, thin compartment. Later, undigested food moves to a second, thick-walled section. Pits, seeds and nuts ground softer foods to a pulp, much like grit does in a bird's gizzard. Digested food is absorbed. Undigested waste is removed as scat. In berry season, the bear can pass fifteen scat-piles a day. Mountain ash berries produce bright red patties. Ecologically, though, a bear is a great gardener, replanting and dispersing seeds, naturally rich in compost, over its wide-foraging range.

Black bear eating mountain ash berries in Clingmans Dome parking lot, fall 2011. *Photo by the author.*

For a bear, Clingmans' menu was inadequate. Acorns and nuts pack the most calories per bite, but hickories and oaks don't grow at six thousand feet. Her search was on. Biologists in the Smokies call it the "fall shuffle." Bears shuffle outside of their home range, hunting high-calorie, protein-rich acorns to build up fat reserves quickly. Some travel over sixty miles. Some years, acorns were plentiful. Other years were disappointing.

In GSMNP, 2011 was a lean year. Food shortage was severe. Berries didn't ripen well, and acorns were scarce. Bears found a limited supply of acorns in the C-loop of Cades Cove Campground. Closing that area to fall-color, leaf-looker tourists for the first time in park history, Chief Wildlife Biologist Bill Stiver and his staff allowed hungry bears to have unlimited access to forage, undisturbed, on a healthy stand of red oak trees. Had the four-year-old female from Clingmans Dome gone that far?

Round and ready, the Dome female returned home. The time had come. Summertime heart rates of eighty-five beats per minute had fallen to fifty-five. Daytime naps were common, her energy more sluggish. Decades ago, a massive red spruce had fallen in a severe windstorm beside the Appalachian Trail, decomposing slowly in high-elevation elements. Its upturned root structure sprawled like arms of an octopus. Curved claws scraped out her den underneath the tangles. Ripping rhododendron and spruce branches into a soft, spongy mass, she lined her bed. Heavy paws raked in old flower stalks and fallen leaves.

Black bears choose to den-up under logs, large boulders, rocky overhangs or knotted brush piles. Some tunnel below the earth in a hole just large enough to allow entry. In GSMNP, however, bears choose uncommon denning sites. Tall, hollow trees are preferred.

Black Bear Research in Great Smoky Mountains National Park

By Jared S. Laufenberg, Department of Forestry, Wildlife and Fisheries, University of Tennessee, 274 Ellington Plant Sciences Building, Knoxville, TN, 37996

The American black bear is the most common of the North American ursids and once occurred in forested habitats from northern Canada into Mexico. Black bears are large omnivorous mammals well adapted to survive in a variety of habitat types. However, bear populations are sensitive to variation in the environment and humans caused a loss of habitat. Since European settlement, the historic range of the black bear has been reduced by nearly 40 percent, with most of that reduction occurring in the conterminous United States. Today, relatively large contiguous populations continue to persist in remote and undeveloped areas, such as the southern Appalachian Mountains.

In the 1960s, wildlife managers were concerned with apparent declines of bear populations in the southern Appalachians and causes of those declines. Those interests led to a collaborative effort between Great Smoky Mountains National Park and the Department of Forestry, Wildlife and Fisheries at the University of Tennessee to assess the status of the bear population in the Smokies. In 1969, Dr. Michael Pelton, a wildlife professor at the University of Tennessee, initiated research to determine the size of the bear population in the Smokies. That research continued for nearly forty years, becoming the longest ongoing American black bear research program of its time.

When Dr. Pelton began his work, information on black bear natural history and how bear populations responded to environmental stresses and human impacts on the landscape was sparse. From the original goal of estimating population size grew a comprehensive research program focusing on population dynamics but extending to the study of many other aspects of bear ecology and research, including habitat use, denning ecology, food habits, research techniques and human-bear interactions. Only through long-term research of bears in the Smokies have researchers been able to provide valuable information for the better management of black bears in the southern Appalachians and beyond.

In GSMNP, Dr. Michael Pelton and other biologists at the University of Tennessee–Knoxville conducted one of the most extensive, longest-running black bear research projects in North America. For nearly forty years, hundreds of bears were tracked, captured, tagged, measured and counted. Research taught them what bears eat, how far they roam, how many there were and where they den. Most important, university and GSMNP studies helped them develop better bear management plans. Humans would stay safe. Wild bears could stay wild.

Radio collars placed on captured bears in the summer led researchers to winter denning sites. Of Smoky bears, they found that 80 percent spent their winters curled up in the hole of a dead tree thirty to eighty feet above ground. Shredded bark provided bedding. Tucked high in a tree cavity, carved by decay after lightning splintered its woody core, a bear snoozed, contentedly.

In March 2002, radio signals led UT graduate students to hibernating female bears. Two cubs, orphaned by a forest fire, each needed a foster mother. Denning season was ending soon. Spring was coming. A mother bear with cubs of her own was more likely to accept an unfamiliar cub in her den.

Dangling from the tip of a long stick, one orphan was placed in a ground den of a mother with two cubs near White Oak Sinks. Instinctively, she accepted the new arrival as one of her own.

Jared Laufenberg, bear biologist/researcher at University of Tennessee–Knoxville, with radio-tracking equipment. *Courtesy of Jared Laufenberg.*

A University of Tennessee–Knoxville researcher tracks a bear to her sixty-five-foot-high tree den in 2007. Fifteen females were tracked that year as part of a long-term study. Over time, biologists learned how many cubs were born to each mother, how well the cubs survived, how often mothers became pregnant, etc. *Courtesy of Jared Laufenberg and www.fieldtripearth.org with North Carolina Zoo Society.*

Foster placement of the second cub was more challenging. With climbing ropes and boot spikes, a graduate student monkeyed up an old chestnut oak tree like a logger. Rope and pulley lifted an orphan in a net up too. Vapor rub applied to his head masked human scent. Carefully, he was lowered inside. Within fifteen minutes, the mother repositioned her cubs for the newcomer to nurse.

By mid-December, temperatures plunged on Clingmans Dome. Howling winds frequently swirled snowflakes. The female bear crawled into her den. Unlike a hibernating chipmunk, whose body temperature drops to freezing (thirty-two degrees Fahrenheit), a bear's temperature only drops a few degrees. Chipmunks wake up every few weeks, raise their body temperatures to normal, eat stored nuts, relieve themselves, lower their temperatures again and return to bed. Black bears sleep without eating, drinking or passing waste for the next five months.

Coarse outer hairs covered thick, wooly inner ones for insulation. Sounds of backcountry winter hikers aroused her senses. Too much disturbance could prompt her to find another den. Sensing no threat to her safety, the female drifted back asleep.

In late January, a movement disturbed her sleep. Wearily, she became more alert and restless. Venturing outside, she scraped in more bedding. Within twenty-four hours, she'd given birth to two cubs. In a small den underneath the protective cover of the old red spruce, the twins curled beside mom for warmth. Unable to hear, see or smell and nearly naked, the pair crawled to mother to nurse. Licked clean and dry, and sheltered from the weather, the twins settled in.

The female had mated in June with several males. Each cub could have different fathers. Fertilized eggs were formed but did not attach to the lining of mother's womb like most mammals. Nature had another plan for black bears. Fertilized eggs remain unattached. Availability of fall food decides their fate. If mother gained enough weight to sustain her health, her pregnancy and the production of milk for cubs, an egg would attach and develop into a cub. With more calories and weight gain, she may deliver one to five offspring. With an acorn-deficient harvest or poor weight gain, eggs may be reabsorbed. Next June, she'd mate again.

Cubs, born the size of squirrels, grew quickly. Mother's milk fat of 35 percent was three times as rich as human's milk. Large baby-blue eyes opened around six weeks. Eventually, they turn brown. Gray fuzz became deep brown or black fur. Above ground, the world was turning green again. Five-pound cubs followed mother from their den in late April.

Lean and hungry, Mother searched for food. Curious cubs explored and played. By example and experiment but mostly instinct, they learned to strip bark, tear up logs, dig for roots and turn over rocks. Fresh, spring shoots were tasty. Ants and grubs provided protein.

Green grass and dandelions along Clingmans Dome Road were tempting, but roadside foraging put the family at risk of passing motorists. Misunderstood threats could prompt mother to stomp, huff and bluff a charge at curious intruders. Recognizing the signs, cubs climbed the nearest fir tree. Man, bobcats and other bears posed the greatest threats to young cubs.

Above: Bear cub crossing Clingmans Dome Road in September 2011. *Photo by the author.*

Opposite, top: A biologist assesses a cub in winter 2007. *Courtesy of Jared Laufenberg.*

Opposite, bottom: Cub and mom foraging along Clingmans Dome Road in September 2011. *Photo by the author.*

As seasons progressed and diets changed, the cubs learned the ways of the wild. In early winter, Mother and cubs denned-up together for another cold season, choosing a new den. Next June, the family parted. She was ready to mate again.

The forty- to fifty-pound siblings separated, searching for new homes. The female yearling foraged nearby, choosing to stay near her mother's territory. For a while, the male wandered over Clingmans Dome. He explored Mount Buckley, down the Appalachian Trail to Goshen Prong and Elkmont. Half a million acres of Smoky Mountains were out there to explore, to stake a claim and, in a few years, to find a mate.

Perhaps when you're in the Smokies and drive down Newfound Gap Road en route to Clingmans Dome, or you take the loop road at Cades Cove, you'll spot a black bear. Maybe its home was Clingmans Dome, or perhaps it's still searching.

Give him space. Love him at a distance. Love him for who he is. Bears just want to be bears.

A University of Tennessee–Knoxville bear study helped NPS biologists develop new bear management policies. NPS volunteers Steve Higdon and Jim Harman prompt a more distant bear-to-visitor experience near Clingmans Dome Visitor Center in April 2011. *Photo by the author.*

CHAPTER 8

BUILDING A MOUNTAIN

The visitor to the Great Smoky Mountains sees at first the predominant forest and the shaded undergrowth, and is not immediately aware that the soils of the forest conceal a solid core of native rock. Later, he notices here and there rocky cliffs and crests...and the great boulders...that are strewn over the mountainsides and choke each rushing torrent. He may then perceive that the rock formations, although masked by soil and vegetation, have determined the fundamental features of the mountain landscape...
—*Arthur Stupka, GSMNP naturalist, and Phillip B. King, geologist; co-authors of "The Great Smoky Mountains—Their Geology and Natural History" in* Scientific Monthly, *1950*

Some barely notice them with a passing glance. Others marvel at their massive size and beauty. The young (and young at heart) pose before cameras beside smooth, coarse-grained surfaces to record park memories. Visitors weary of mind, or just weary of feet, find a rocky perch on boulders at Clingmans Dome parking lot and rest.

What's underneath the hands and knees, the derrière and foot? How did these giant boulders get here? What's in the rock? What influence does that have on the ecosystem, on what grows and lives here? How old is Clingmans Dome and the Great Smoky Mountains? How were these mountains formed?

Some answers lie within the rocks themselves. The rock type and texture attest to an origin beneath deep waters. The rocks on Clingmans Dome, the highest mountain in Great Smoky Mountain National Park, used to be on the bottom of an ancient ocean.

Return to the days before saber-toothed tigers, wooly mammoths, giant sloths and other mammals roamed the valleys of the Smoky Mountains. Return to a land without birds, flowers, reptiles or even insects. Find a moonscape, a barren world void of color and life as we know it. Only primitive creatures lived here.

Rains washed sediments, eroding from an ancient landmass, into streams and rivers. Mud, silt and pebbles were transported by water, dumping some of its load into deep oceans. Sediments sank, piling up layer upon layer. Under mounting weight and pressure, grains and particles were squeezed together. Tightly pressed for millions of years, sand, silt and pebble became solid, sedimentary rocks on the ocean floor. In the ocean depths, hundreds to thousands of feet beneath the surface, the rocks on Clingmans Dome were born.

About one billion years ago, Earth's continents were positioned near the equator, forming a supercontinent called Rodinia. Heat radiating from the planet's core created rotating convection currents in the earth's mantle, helping move the tectonic plates of land and sea floor. Eventually, Rodinia broke apart as continental plates drifted away from each other.

Millions of years passed. Continents on broken tectonic plates of the earth's crust, in what is now Europe and Africa, drifted toward tectonic plates in the Western Hemisphere. Inching toward one another, they began to collide some four hundred million years ago. Land was added to present New England and the Canadian Maritime Provinces. Further collisions created the Northern Appalachians.

South America and Africa (known as Gondwana) collided with North America (known as Laurentia), forming a supercontinent called Pangea. About 230 million years ago, the last collision, a period known as the Allegheny orogeny (meaning: "mountain building"), formed the southern Appalachians, home of GSMNP.

Landmass crunched landmass. Horizontal plates buckled. Continuous pressures wrinkled, folded and cracked layers of rock. Older rocks were pushed up and over younger rocks. Over millions of years, mountains were elevated. In a northeast-to-southwest direction, the Appalachian Mountain chain formed. Today, the Appalachians still lie in that orientation, inland, but parallel to the Atlantic coastline. Geologists speculate that Clingmans Dome and other high peaks in the region were once many times their current altitude.

Highest Mountain in the Great Smokies

During one of these continental collisions, the rock mass of Clingmans Dome and the Smoky Mountains changed forever. Subjected to intense heat and pressure, sedimentary rocks changed to metamorphic rocks. Rocks on Clingmans Dome that retained some sedimentary features are classified as meta-sandstone. Meta-conglomerates at the Dome consist of metamorphic rocks of sand and pebbles.

Time advanced. Pangea's surface split. Tensional stress, concentrated at continental plate margins, pulled the landmasses apart. Like a knife slicing a pie, deep cuts separated them. The North American plate drifted west, and the North African drifted east to their positions seen on a globe today. The rift valley between them filled with water that became the Atlantic Ocean. One half of the valley's edge remained attached to the continent moving west and the other half to the one going east.

Evidence exists that the continents were once joined. Rock types on continents an ocean apart are similar. The Atlas and Lesser Atlas Mountains, across the northwest edge of Africa, are twin sisters to the Appalachians. Fossils of amphibians and plants are similar. The jagged edges of the continents could be roughly pieced back together like patterns on a quilt.

Although the continents have settled in place as seen today, nature continues to sculpt, mold and reshape the landscape. Heavy rains cascade down steep slopes, forcing particles to tumble in turbulent waters. Rocks and pebbles grind against one another, sanding away rough surfaces. Gravity rules and weather contributes. Harsh winters freeze water droplets in tiny cracks. Warmer temperatures thaw ice and snow, expanding cracks into deeper cuts. Erosion chisels landscape, rock and mountain. Rock surfaces split and eventually sever, causing tiny fragments to fall from their ancient holds in parent rock.

Over time, topography readjusted. Mountains got new faces, new slopes and new designs. Higher terrain and steeper inclines caused streams to flow faster and stronger. River courses found new routes.

Then glaciers changed everything. Approximately eighteen thousand years ago, the most recent glacial period, called the Wisconsin Glacial Episode, held much of Canada and the northern United States icebound. For thousands of years, the ice front crept southward into Ohio and Pennsylvania. As centuries passed, climates warmed and the ice sheet receded. Cold cycles returned, advancing the ice flow again. Wax and wane, warm then cold, interglacial periods alternated with frozen ones. Today, in the north, glacial deposits remain. Polished by grit and furrowed by stone, grooves in a rock outcrop in Central Park, New York, permanently preserve a glacial history.

Thunderhead sandstone in Clingmans Dome Parking Lot. Summer 2012. *Photo by the author.*

Glaciers did not make it to the Great Smoky Mountains. Most likely, though, snowfields packed recessed hollows on Clingmans Dome. Alpine tundra and subarctic vegetation grew on open slopes. Canadian boreal forests of fir and spruce inhabited lower slopes. Hardwoods dominated the valleys.

As glaciers advanced, sand, silt, pebble and rock forged ahead of the massive ice sheet, grinding surface against surface. Bedrock surfaces were exposed. Pennsylvania, Virginia, North Carolina and other areas south of the ice front endured severely cold climates. Temperatures hovered around thirty-two degrees Fahrenheit. Daytime temperatures could cause melting, but bitterly cold nights formed new ice. Extended periods of warmer weather were often followed by cold spells. Even massive, resistant rocks could not withstand the repeated pressures of freeze and thaw, freeze and thaw.

Melted snows seeped down into cracks in the bedrock. Trapped water froze, expanding the cracks. Crack by crack, thousands of years of freezing and thawing fractured mountainsides. Blocks of giant boulders, some the size of an RV, parted from their rocky foundations. Gravity pulled. Rocks slowly moved downslope. While some slid, others rolled, exposing more of its rock surface to weather. They split again. Rivers in the watershed valleys below Clingmans Dome still hold relics of an ancient climate. Time has removed sand, mud and silt, leaving displaced rocks and boulders to churn placid water into eddies. Clear water swirls into white foam.

As the region began its final warming trend about fifteen thousand years ago, Canadian conifers migrated up to the higher elevations of the Southern Appalachians. Hardwoods grew in coves on sheltered slopes, while a wide range of plants rooted in valleys. Forests grew.

During the past ten thousand years, environmental forces have continued to sand away at rock surfaces. Crevices in the rockface and gaps between boulders have collected organic matter. Rooted herbaceous plants widen the cracks, causing portions to break. Rock and debris slide down steep mountain slopes. Flash floods accelerate the movement.

Years of weathering have left highly resistant Thunderhead sandstone exposed along the highest peaks of the Smokies, including Clingmans Dome. Named for the rocks exposed on Thunderhead Mountain, west of Clingmans Dome, Thunderhead sandstone is a coarse-grained, light gray, cliff-forming rock as much as five thousand to six thousand feet thick. Pebbly conglomerates and blue quartz, characteristic of Thunderhead, can be seen. Siltstone and shale are imbedded. Many waterfalls in the park, such as Laurel Falls and Rainbow Falls, plunge over tough, resistant Thunderhead sandstone.

Pause to survey the Thunderhead sandstone outcrops that border the parking lot at Clingmans Dome. Look for concretion circles. Like pressed snowballs plastered into a soft snow bank, hardened, compact circles are scattered across the rocky surfaces. Early in the rock's history, minerals

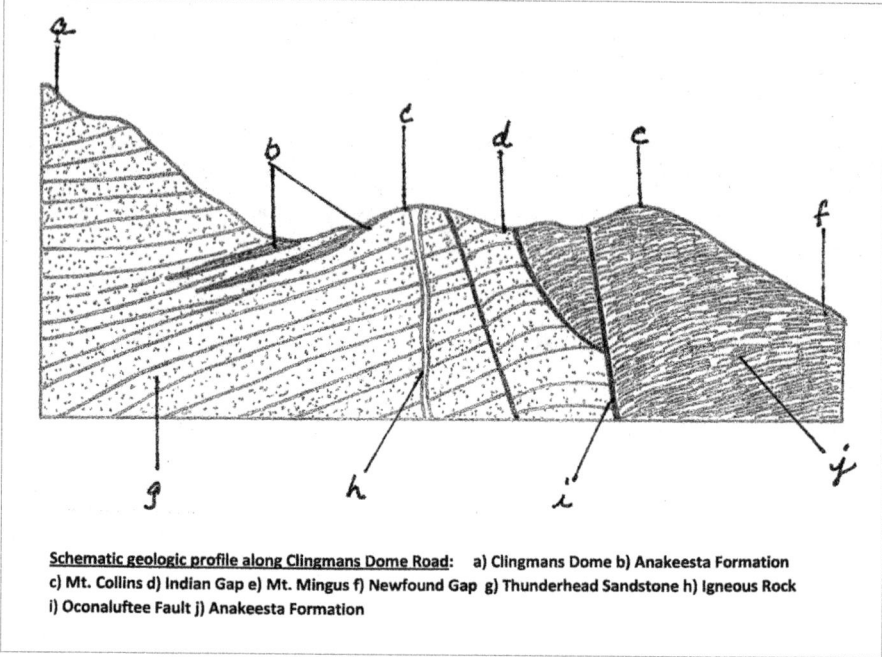

Schematic geologic profile along Clingmans Dome Road: a) Clingmans Dome b) Anakeesta Formation c) Mt. Collins d) Indian Gap e) Mt. Mingus f) Newfound Gap g) Thunderhead Sandstone h) Igneous Rock i) Oconaluftee Fault j) Anakeesta Formation

Illustration by Tim Worsham, drawn with permission from Harry L. Moore, *A Roadside Guide to the Geology of the GSMNP* and University of Tennessee Press.

cemented together into a hardened mass. One ring encircling another formed around a nucleus fragment of black slate. Over time, varying degrees of resistance to erosion and weathering between the sandstone and concretion left the circular formations exposed. Concretions have intrigued people for generations. Early rockhounds thought they were dinosaur eggs, fossils or relics from an ancient culture. Perhaps Clingmans' concretions could be considered birthmarks.

Milky-white quartz filling fractures dissects some rock outcrops. Deep gashes crisscross, parallel and zigzag through the rock mass. Light colored feldspar, a mineral that forms 60 percent of the world's crust, is also found in Thunderhead sandstone.

A long, thin segment of metamorphosed igneous rock, called an intrusion, is found north of Clingmans Dome. Underground intrusions form dikes. More than 480 million years ago, magma at the Earth's core was intruded as "liquid" molten rock into a fissure. When temperatures cooled, the magma hardened in the dike. Underfoot, on the connector path to Sugarland

Mountain Trail (3.5 miles west on Clingmans Dome Road), lies the small igneous dike. Soil deposits and vegetative overgrowth limit a good view.

Although Thunderhead sandstone is the most common rock structure beneath the Dome, rocks of the Anakeesta Formation are also noted. Unlike the massive gray sandstone weathered to rounded boulders and sandstone cliffs, the acidic, shale-like, dark-colored Anakeesta are thin, slaty rocks. Weathering exposes an iron sulfide mineral called pyrite. Pyrite can resemble gold. However, while pyrite cannot be scratched with a knife, gold can. Even a penny will scratch gold. Pyrite, or "fool's gold," in contact with air and water turns rock surfaces to a rusty color and can form a sulfuric acid runoff that lowers the stream ph to detrimental levels.

Compare outcrops of Anakeesta with Thunderhead along Clingmans Dome Road and Trail. Strata of the Anakeesta Formation are more prevalent on Chimney Tops and Mount Le Conte. The name comes from the impressive Anakeesta Ridge seen on the popular Alum Cave Trail on the southwest face of Mount Le Conte. Chimney Tops, climbed by many and seen by anyone who drives Newfound Gap Road, are magnificent twin spires of Anakeesta Formation.

Take note as you drive through Indian Gap on Clingmans Dome Road. Here the Road Prong Trail (an old wagon road) roughly follows the ancient, dormant Oconaluftee Fault, one of the major faults in the park. Branching off the Gatlinburg Fault, the Oconaluftee Fault crosses the crest of the Smokies. A fault line occurs where rock surfaces are broken apart and displaced during tectonic plate movement. Traversing a northwest–southeast direction, the fault line crosses into North Carolina through the Oconaluftee Valley along the Oconaluftee River.

Earth is a dynamic place. Even rock foundations are moving. Rockslides are obvious. But most movement goes unnoticed. Unlike the seasonal flowering of a Michaux's saxifrage clinging to a tiny bit of rocky turf deposited by a local lichen; and unlike the visual display of the crisp air of autumn warning hardwood trees to shut down food production, discontinue chlorophyll, and unmask their true colors; or unlike the progressive demise of a dense Fraser fir forest at the destructive hands of human folly, most rock movements are imperceptible. Inches a year, however, we're still drifting.

Whether you perch on, pass by or just simply stroke the Thunderhead sandstone as you ascend the Clingmans Dome Trail, know that you are in the presence of some of the oldest rocks in the region. What was once at the bottom of an ocean has been folded, faulted, metamorphosed, uplifted, chipped, cracked and sanded by time and elements. Clingmans Dome now

Clingmans Dome

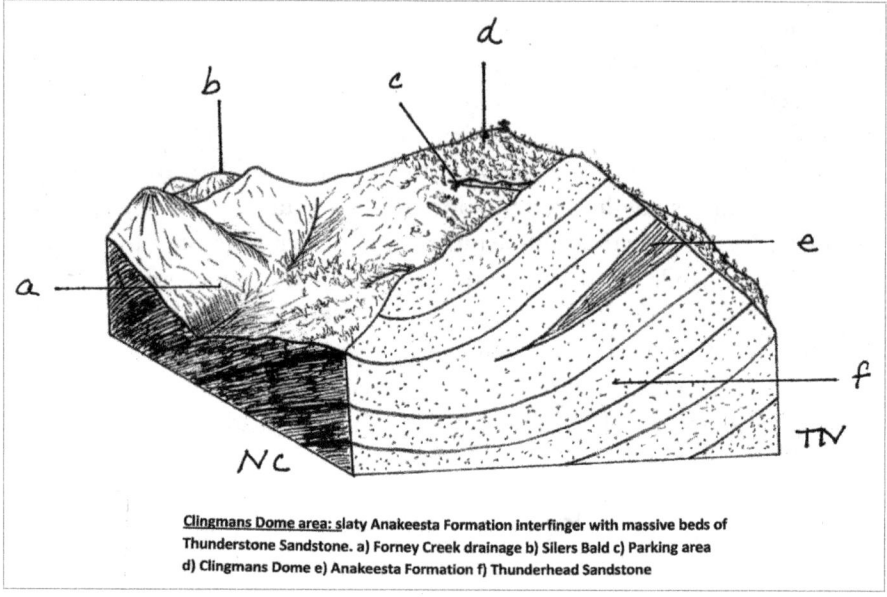

Clingmans Dome area: slaty Anakeesta Formation interfinger with massive beds of Thunderstone Sandstone. a) Forney Creek drainage b) Silers Bald c) Parking area d) Clingmans Dome e) Anakeesta Formation f) Thunderhead Sandstone

Illustration by Tim Worsham, drawn with permission from Harry L. Moore, *A Roadside Guide to the Geology of the GSMNP* and University of Tennessee Press.

lifts its head above the backbone of the Smokies. Bit by bit, though, water droplets take it back. Its sandy quartz chips, over the years, will migrate back, traveling creeks and rivers to the mighty Mississippi River on its way to the Gulf of Mexico. Next time you stand on a Gulf Coast beach, scoop up a handful of soft, white sand, and remember the Dome!

CHAPTER 9
MONITORING AIR AND WATER

"There's nothing else I can do for you," a doctor might have said in 1890, "except to offer some advice. Move to the mountains. Breathe the fresh, cool air. Rest and recuperate there."

Before the discovery of an antibiotic for tuberculosis, physicians prescribed therapeutic mountain air for patients suffering from TB and other breathing difficulties. Open-air porches and mountain terraces built at sanitariums around the world boasted the healing power of clean mountain air.

Sadly, over the last hundred years, progress has changed the quality of air. Human population grew. More people meant more cars. Demands for greater conveniences and more products increased. Factories expanded to supply the demands, and power plants burned more fuel to generate enough electricity to meet the factories' needs.

The cheapest, most readily available fuel source was coal. It still is. In 2011, 49 percent of U.S. electricity was powered by nonrenewable coal. Created by ancient, dead plants subjected to eons of extreme pressure, coal beds are mined in twenty-six states, primarily Wyoming, West Virginia, Kentucky, Pennsylvania and Montana. Unfortunately for the Southern Appalachians, though, coal on fire releases dirty smoke, a smoke that contains carbon dioxide, sulfur, nitrogen, mercury and other pollutants. The world wanted modern conveniences but was blindly paying dearly for it—breath by breath.

Smoke drifts to the Smokies. Winds in temperate regions of North America mostly travel west to east, carrying pollutants with them. Midwest factories and power plants are less affected by their own toxic smoke than areas downwind. Plants, animals and people in the Smokies sit in its flight path, and GSMNP acts as a barricade to prevailing winds. Pollutants park and persist here.

Up and over massive mountains, winds push eastward. As air rises and cools, water droplets condense and form misty clouds. Like a giant kapok tree in the Amazon rainforest, Clingmans Dome is often soaked in drippy, humid mists. Dome mists, though, are tainted with sulfates and nitrates emitted from smokestacks. These elements combine with water droplets forming strong acids called acid deposition, or acid rain.

Acid rain can cause precipitation in GSMNP to be five to ten times more acidic than normal rainfall. Clingmans Dome receives twenty-five more inches than the valleys below. More rain means greater exposures to acids. Half the time, the Dome sits in a cloud with an average pH of 3.6—as acidic as vinegar.

"Air that acidic alters the natural soil and stream chemistry, which harms plant and animal life," says Jim Renfro, air quality specialist for GSMNP. Renfro has been monitoring the air quality in the park for decades.

Ground-level ozone, or smog (not the high-level ozone layer that protects Earth from harmful sun rays), also contributes to air pollution. Nitrogen oxides are emitted from power plants and factories, but motor vehicles and non-road engines are worse. Another emitted chemical, volatile organic compounds (VOC), mixes with nitrogen oxides. Together, in sunlight, they form a toxic gas. Matt Kulp, fisheries biologist for GSMNP, reports that the Smokies receive some of the highest nitrate deposition of anywhere in North America, much of it from vehicle emissions.

According to the Environmental Protection Agency, Americans traveled 178 percent more miles, in 210 million vehicles, between 1970 and 2005 than in previous decades. By 2000, drivers were choosing larger vehicles (vans, SUVs, heavy trucks), which burn more fuel and emit more chemicals. Larger vehicles pollute three to five times more than smaller cars. In GSMNP, where an estimated nine million people visit annually, an average of 350 personnel work regularly and more than three thousand volunteers routinely serve, a lot of engine-generated toxic gas is created.

The invisible, airborne toxic chemicals in ground-level ozone clog plant pores, preventing photosynthesis and food production. Human airways are harmed. Sunlight intensifies ozone, cooking it in summer to dangerous levels. Clingmans Dome is particularly vulnerable at night. Ground-level ozone from lower elevations, like Knoxville, rises to the level of a cooler, mountaintop layer of air but doesn't pass through it. Toxic ozone blankets Clingmans Dome all night.

Tiny particulate matter (dust, smoke, silt, etc.), suspended in air, hinders visibility. Depth of field, clarity and distance are reduced. Steamy summer air makes it worse.

Atop Clingmans Dome, the National Park Service operates the highest air quality monitoring station in the east. Erected in 1993, this monitoring station is one of seven in the park. (Others are Elkmont, Cove Mountain, Cades Cove, Purchase Knob, Look Rock and Noland Divide.) Research and data from the Dome's comprehensive system have determined the source of toxic gases: primarily, industries in the Midwest and the Southeast. The system measures ozone, acid levels, weather, solar radiation and other elements. Like the monitoring station at Elkmont, a mercury monitoring system funnels precipitation into a collection box. A lab in Seattle analyzes the contents monthly, comparing high-elevation levels collected at Clingmans Dome to those of lower altitudes, like Elkmont.

A misty Clingmans Dome. *Photo by the author.*

Clingmans Dome, Tennessee, and Whiteface Mountain, New York, were the only stations in the east that had automated cloud collectors. Budget shortfalls in 2012 meant cloud analysis at the Dome had to end. However, cloud collectors had shown that over half of the acid deposition on the Dome came from clouds. Through research and networking, these sites have analyzed and compared data on pH, specific conductance, nitrate, sulfate, chloride, calcium, magnesium, potassium, sodium and ammonium. Wind direction and speed, air temperature and humidity, barometric pressures and liquid water content were also noted.

Real-time hourly readings of ground-level ozone are assessed. The National Park Service issues warnings when the levels are dangerously elevated. Children, the elderly and those with chronic respiratory illness

Air quality monitoring station atop Clingmans Dome. *Illustration by Tim Worsham.*

should especially take heed. A *green* ozone warning indicates no threat, *yellow* means exercise caution and *orange* indicates one should choose a lower elevation to hike.

In December 1952, air pollution became recognized as a health hazard. London was gripped in an icy winter. Bitter cold fog enveloped the city for months. Heaps of coal fed fires for warmth. Black smoke billowed continuously, embracing the city in the stationary cold layer of air. The invisible concentration of toxins accumulated to dangerous levels. Densely polluted air entered buildings. Theater performances were cancelled because patrons could not see the stage. By March, four thousand people had died. Eight thousand more died over the following months. Cause of death: air pollution.

London's "Killer Smog" and other similar events in the United States led to a global awareness of air pollution. The first U.S. Clean Air Act was written in 1963 and updated in 1970, when the Environmental Protection Agency (EPA) was born. In 1990, the EPA imposed stricter air quality guidelines and currently reevaluates new scientific data that warrants updated measures.

Reductions in the emission of poisonous gases were critical. New industrial policies were imposed. Smokestack scrubbers sprayed wet limestone powder onto burning coal, absorbing sulfur from gases. Other factories considered washing specks of sulfur from coal before burning it. Soaking in a vat of water, coal particles sink, sulfur floats. Another option is to separate sulfur molecules from those of coal. Chemically "glued" together, it's hard to do. Scientists continue testing ways to economically separate the two in the future.

Other improved measures include newer, pressurized coal boilers that burn coal at lower temperatures. Much less sulfur and nitrogen oxide gases are formed.

The U.S. Department of Energy recommends changing coal rocks into coal gases by breaking apart their atoms. Burn coal gases to generate electricity, not chunks of coal rock. After filtration, very few toxic elements remain in gaseous coal.

Nitrogen oxides can also be reduced by burning coal in stages. The Clean Coal Technology Program believes that 75 percent of coal-burning boilers will soon be designed with this feature.

Catalytic converters have improved nitrogen oxide gases emitted from automobiles. Both diesel and gasoline fuels are cleaner. Car dealers are selling smaller cars. Other clean air measures include electrostatic air cleaners to remove unhealthy particles in the air. Dust particles adhere to electrically charged plates, much like lint adheres to a computer screen. Further research hopes to provide feasible ways to reduce carbon dioxide and mercury emissions.

Each week, Jim Renfro and crew visit all seven air quality monitoring stations. "We've been monitoring these sites every second of every minute for the past thirty years," Renfro states. He has assisted hundreds of researchers from around the world studying the effects of air pollutants on ecosystems.

"In everything we do," he explains, "our mission is to protect, preserve and pass it on to the next generation un-impaired." The NPS participates in research, monitoring, education and collaboration to meet air quality standards imposed by the EPA. Staff at GSMNP act as regional advisors to other state and local areas wanting to improve their air quality too.

Records show that smokestack scrubbers and gasoline-emission controls on automobiles have improved conditions dramatically in the Smokies. Sulfur emissions have decreased 75 percent since 1990. Nitrogen oxides are down 70 percent. Ground-level ozone in the park is down 30 percent; acid rain, 25 percent.

Particulate matter in the atmosphere is reduced. Visibility at the park has improved 99 percent over the past decade. In 1998 on an average hazy day, visitors could see a maximum of nine miles; in 2009, one could see twenty-four miles.

Pollution levels have improved, but what about the quality of life? Can vegetation recover from long-term effects? What major impacts do air pollutants have on the spruce-fir forest ecosystem? What's at risk on Clingmans Dome? What about human health?

Inhabitants at high elevations are injured the most. Acid rain is especially cruel to red spruce. "Red spruce and Fraser fir branches," says Renfro, "act like little bottle-brushes efficiently collecting pollutants out of the air and clouds." Ninety plant species in the park have shown leaf damage from high ozone levels. Most damage has been noted in higher elevations.

Purplish-brown spots on upper surfaces of lower leaves on cutleaf coneflower (*Rudbeckia lacinata*) indicate ozone damage. A two-year study completed in 2001, "Ozone Injury on Cutleaf Coneflower…in GSMNP" (by Chappelka, Neufeld, Davison, Somers and Renfro), was the first scientific report of the severity of ozone injury to these plants. Study plots beside Clingmans Dome Trail, Cherokee Orchard Road and at Purchase Knob were observed. Ozone injury was significant and by far the greatest on cutleaf coneflowers growing on Clingmans Dome.

In 2001, bio-monitoring gardens were planted at Twin Creeks, Tremont and Purchase Knob to study vegetative effects from pollution. Data from the low-elevation sites, Twin Creeks and Tremont, is being compared with data collected from high-elevation Purchase Knob.

Clingmans Dome dominates the headwaters of many mountain streams. Like garden rows tilled by a devoted farmer, parallel creeks wind their way down deep crevices on its northern slopes. The waters merge to form the Little River, the park's longest river. Those waters flow into the Tennessee River, the largest tributary of the Ohio. "Tanasi," some say, is named for a former Cherokee village.

Precipitation falling on its southern slopes flow into Forney, Deep and Noland Creeks. Each flows into the Tuckasegee River near Bryson City, North Carolina. Beneath the backwaters of Fontana Lake, the Tuckaseegee joins the Little Tennessee River. Those waters dump into the Tennessee River to reunite with waters drained from the Dome's north flank. Six hundred miles later, all merge with the Ohio en route to the Mississippi and the Gulf of Mexico.

Resting entirely within the Tennessee watershed and furnishing gallons of water to mountain valleys, Clingmans' health affects the quality of life in the streams it feeds. Rain purges impurities from the atmosphere. Toxins percolate through layers of soil and enter groundwater, creeks and streams. Tainted streams affect rivers. Accumulated pollutants travel to the Gulf and are swept out to sea by ocean currents.

After a heavy storm when toxic pollutants are washed from the atmosphere, stream pH in the Smokies can be as toxic as 4.0, too acidic for native fish, salamanders and insects. A healthy stream has a pH of six or seven. During a flash flood, a sudden, severe flush of acid water can kill some species immediately.

Matt Kulp has managed water quality monitoring programs in the Smokies since 1993. "Acid rain," Kulp says, "is the major issue with water quality in the park." Thirty sites are sampled every two months in seven watersheds. Twelve streams on the Tennessee side of the park, Kulp says, are too impure to meet Clean Water Act mandates. (Currently, North Carolina stream data is unavailable.) Clean water is dependent on clean air. "It's the other half of the battle," said Renfro.

Persistent acid rain causes nitrogen to accumulate in soils. On Clingmans Dome, nitrogen is 80 percent greater than normal. Excessive nitrogen removes phosphorous, magnesium, calcium and aluminum from the soil. Plants lose valuable nutrients needed for healthy growth. Aluminum changes to a toxic metal that disrupts electrolyte levels in streams.

Reduced calcium weakens snail shells as well as bird eggs. Research biologists study the effects of diminished calcium on songbirds that migrate back to breed in the higher elevations. Breeding success and population numbers will be evaluated. Others have studied the impact of air and water pollution on the resident dark-eyed junco.

Industries have made positive changes to improve air quality. The EPA is watching. So are environmentalists. Jim Renfro, Matt Kulp and the National Park Service are dedicated to ongoing research and monitoring to assess effectiveness of current air quality control measures, as well as the need for further improvements. What can mere mortals do?

Hike more; drive less. Carpool. Combine errands. Drive cleaner fuel-burning vehicles. Electric is even better. Renfro says, "Every extra part per billion reduced out of everyone's tail pipe would make a difference."

Limit use of foam plastic cups, charcoal lighter fluid, house paints and hair spray, all of which contribute to air pollution. Reduce wood burning; update to cleaner wood stoves and fireplaces. Burn only dry, seasoned wood. Ignite less often.

Reduce thermostats. Choose fluorescent lights; switch off TVs; insulate. Stay informed. Have an opinion. Care. Follow updates and air quality trends at www.epa.gov/air and the National Park Service web page: www.nps.gov. See current issues in Clean Air Technology at the U.S. Department of Energy: www.eia.gov/.

On April 7, 1869, Thomas L. Clingman wrote, "Even the balsam fir tree, which is usually of no great height, attains an altitude of one hundred and fifty feet on the southern side of the Great Smoky [Clingmans Dome]...The fact that the mountains become richer as we ascend is doubtless due to... [the fact that they're] often enveloped by clouds, and kept cool and moist..."

Air, water and soils are sick right now, Mr. Clingman. Lessons have been learned, though, and emotions and brains stirred into action. Problems are being addressed. The future is hopeful.

U.S. Senator Bill Frist (R-TN) and EPA director Christine Todd Whitman came to the Smokies in July 2002 to witness its air quality firsthand. Jim Renfro was their guide. *Smoky Mountain News* covered the story. The newspaper reported that Renfro told the senator and the EPA, "We [GSMNP] want to be at the table" when air quality policies are being discussed.

Fifty activists arrived at Clingmans Dome that day, wearing gas masks and carrying signs that read, "Smoggy Mountains." The EPA director pointed toward the crowd, saying, "Those protestors out there...we're on the same side."

One large table, many passionate voices, a single goal.

A healthy adult sitting on a bench beside Clingmans Dome Trail inhales about seven and a half liters of air each minute. That's about three thousand gallons of air a day. An individual ascending three hundred feet in half a mile to the tower at the end of the Dome trail may breathe twenty-five liters or more a minute. The quality of that air is vital to human health and to the health of the plants and animals sharing that ecosystem with us.

One hundred years ago, visitors came to the mountains to restore their health, to breathe in clean, cool mountain air. Can we return the favor? Can we give Clingmans Dome and the surrounding Smoky Mountains their fresh air back?

CHAPTER 10

FOLLOWING A TRAIL

Where can you find the highest trailhead in the Smokies, walk the A.T.'s highest section between Georgia and Maine or climb its highest mountain? Where is the highest grassy bald in GSMNP?

Where can you walk through a forest that smells like home on Christmas Eve? Where's the park's longest water slide, the closest trail shelter to a road and the best scenic view on a clear day? Where can you experience a high-elevation sunrise or sunset? Where can you find twin springs fifty yards apart and a mile high in two different states?

Where is a trail barely wide enough for a gymnast on a balance beam? What trail places one boot-step in North Carolina and the other in Tennessee? Where can you walk the spine of an ancient mountain ridge that was born on the bottom of an ocean? What about mighty boulders with concretions, stones sliced with quartz and large rocks sculpting streams, commanding their courses?

Where's the second-best flame azalea garden in the park? Where are three rare orchids, a lemming, a plant that eats bugs and a rare high-mountain bog? What about a flower, spider and snail found nowhere else in the world? Where's North Carolina's largest yellow birch? How about a trail through forest zones, as if hiking Carolina to Canada? Where is a gorgeous wildflower garden protected from wild boars?

Where can you hike North Carolina's largest altitude drop and one of Tennessee's greatest descents in GSMNP? Where's a pathway that was an ancient Indian trail and then a Civil War path, a livestock route to market

View from Clingmans Dome Road. *Illustration by Tim Worsham.*

and an old wagon road? What trail follows the first route across the Smokies? Where is there a historic railroad grade, remains of a CCC camp and scars of the logging age?

What if you wanted to relive a "Save the Smokies" hike? Or follow in the footsteps of Cherokee Indians, Civil War soldiers, explorers and botanists? What about those of Thomas Clingman, Samuel Buckley or Professor

Guyot? Where can one place boot prints on tread marks left by thousands of feet attempting to hike the A.T.'s 2,100 miles, end-to-end?

Where? Near Clingmans Dome.

Hiking trails radiate from the mountain itself. Others extend and cross Clingmans Dome Road. Popular ones depart from the parking lot. Some trails are looped. Unless shuttle is arranged for one-way, long-distance hiking, some are "in and outers." Most are steep; others are steeper still. Footpaths are often rough, rocky and quite muddy. Remote solitude is frequent. Challenges are inherent, but rewards are immeasurable.

The aim of this text is to inform, enlighten and perhaps entertain. Human and natural history are emphasized more than trail description. Information presented here may entice some visitors to lace-up and explore. But hopefully even the "armchair" hiker will be able to vicariously enjoy the trip.

Excellent trail guidebooks are available in park visitor centers. Hiking guides describe trail terrain, length, degree of difficulty and elevation change. Leave any park trailhead with one in your pocket. A trail map is essential too.

Hiking in high-elevation zones demands extra precautions. Weather in all seasons is unpredictable. Temperatures at Clingmans Dome can be twenty degrees colder than the valleys. Severe summer thunderstorms can appear quickly, and cloud-to-ground lightning is possible. Winds can be fierce.

Prevent hypothermia. Wear layers and pack raingear. Carry water and snacks, and only drink treated water from park streams. Know your own physical capabilities and those of your trail mates. Cell phone signals are erratic in high mountain terrain. Let someone know where you're going. Be smart. Have fun.

Clingmans Dome (CD) Trail

From Clingmans Dome Parking lot, climb three hundred feet for one half mile on an asphalt trail to the summit. The loss of Fraser firs provides distant North Carolina views to Fontana Lake. Open trailside vegetation entices birdwatchers. Struggling spruce and fir dot the landscape that was once a dense, dark forest. Wildflowers bloom summer to fall. In season, thornless blackberries attract wildlife. Flaky, rust-colored Anakeesta and gray Thunderhead boulders border the trail.

Benches along the way suggest a relaxed pace. Thinner air at six thousand feet may require an occasional break. At the crest of the ridge, the trail becomes flatter. On a clear day, a forty-five-foot-tall observation tower offers 360-degree views of GSMNP and beyond.

Appalachian Trail

As the longest marked trail in the United States (more than 2,100 miles), moving through fourteen states from Georgia to Maine, the Appalachian Trail (A.T.) reaches its highest point on Clingmans Dome (6,643 feet). Of the seventy-two A.T. miles in GSMNP, the Dome rests almost mid-point between Fontana Lake and Davenport Gap, straddling the Tennessee–North Carolina state line.

Each year, roughly one thousand "thru-hikers" attempt to hike the A.T. from one end to the other. An estimated one in four complete the journey. Northbound thru-hikers start arriving at the Dome in late April after hiking nearly 230 miles from Springer Mountain, Georgia. Some shuttle from the Clingmans Dome parking lot to nearby towns for beds, showers, steaks and supplies. About five million steps over four to seven months will take them over the Appalachian Range and up that final mountain peak: Mount Katahdin in Maine.

Millions of people each year hike some part of the A.T. "Section hikers" may backpack a portion a week at a time. Scout troops, hiking clubs and family groups adopt a segment, complete it together and move on to another section with the next expedition.

Many enjoy the trail as day hikers. Several day hiker options are available at Clingmans Dome. The Dome's proximity to the A.T. offers all types of hikers access to wilderness areas, without a more adventurous commitment.

A.T./Clingmans Dome Bypass Trail

Make a loop. Ascend the paved Clingmans Dome Trail to the observation platform. On return, leave the rock patio at the base of the tower. Go back along the ridgeline's flat, paved trail to a sign on the right: "Appalachian Trail." Hike 0.3 miles along the A.T. toward Mount Buckley. Rock boulders, wildflowers and spruce-fir forests are highlights. Although unseen, remember that the rare spruce-fir moss spider lives here. Look for colonies of Rugel's Indian plantain.

In a severe, turbulent ice storm in February 1974, a single-engine Cherokee airplane lost power, bringing the plane down on Devil's Courthouse Ridge on the North Carolina side of Mount Buckley. All seven passengers survived.

At the "Bypass Trail" sign, turn left. Descend along a rocky path to the Forney Ridge Trail. Norwood Lumber Company logged this steep mountainside in the 1920s. Turn left at the sign. Hike 0.2 miles back to the parking lot.

Appalachian Trail: Newfound Gap to Clingmans Dome

Paralleling Clingmans Dome Road, this 7.5-mile roller coaster is the highest section of the A.T. Most of this route is over a mile high. Pass giant red spruce trees uprooted in severe, high-mountain windstorms, creating perfect bear dens. Hear blackburnians, brown creepers, winter wrens, veerys, black-throated green warblers and other high-elevation birds. Cringe at the scolding chatter of red squirrels.

Climb a metal ramp across a wire fence, barricading bulldozer-like tusks of wild boars from precious wildflowers. Alternate a Volunteer State step in Tennessee with a Tar Heel one in North Carolina across a narrow ridgeline. Rest on a massive quartz boulder. Whisper in a shadowed red spruce forest. Dense canopies crown straight, bare trunks, poised like saints above hallowed ground. Thick layers of brown needles cover the forest floor like a warm comforter.

Climb Mount Collins, named by Professor Guyot for Robert Collins. In 1859, Collins cleared the path for Guyot to measure the height of Clingmans Dome. In nearby Indian Gap, Mr. Collins collected tolls from farmers driving livestock to local markets along the first road across the Smokies.

Find Mount Collins trail shelter, the closest shelter to any road access in the park. Through volunteer hard labor, all GSMNP backcountry trail shelters have received a facelift. Wooden shelters built by the CCC in the 1930s had burned or deteriorated. Since 1998, stone shelters were constructed, eroded areas filled and leaky structures razed. Helicopters airlifted supplies into remote areas. Heavy rains often hampered progress. Some of the greatest delays occurred at high-elevation Mount Collins.

Continue south along the A.T. toward Clingmans Dome. Signs of the massive destruction and loss of life that occurred here were concealed over

Mount Collins Trail Shelter. A 2013 George B. Hartzog Jr. Award for Outstanding Volunteer Service was presented to the Smoky Mountain Hiking Club Backcountry Shelter Crew. After twenty thousand hours of labor, $750,000 of donated construction items and 120 tons of ground moved, SMHC volunteers had completely renovated all fifteen backcountry trail shelters in GSMNP. *Illustration by Tim Worsham.*

Albert "Dutch" Roth, Carlos Campbell, Guy Frizzell, Myron Avery and Oliver Crowder on a hike from Newfound Gap, over Clingmans Dome, to Deal's Gap, May 29–31, 1931. *Courtesy of Albert "Dutch" Roth Collection, University of Tennessee–Knoxville Libraries.*

time. Sheared treetops and rolled boulders are no longer obvious. Strips of fuselage and wings, contorted pieces of structural framework, cockpit gear and instruments and fragmented bits of aviation metal, strewn a mile wide, have long since been removed.

During a routine night-training military mission returning to Tampa from Chicago on June 12, 1946, a Boeing B-29 Superfortress crashed about three hundred feet below the crest of the Smokies, less than a mile east of Clingmans Dome tower. In Tennessee, just north of the A.T., the bomber nosed into the ground, losing its wings. Speed and weight propelled it over the state line, coming to an explosive, fiery halt one-quarter of a mile into North Carolina, close to Clingmans Dome Road. One of its four engines landed beside the road. All twelve onboard were killed.

On March 30, 2003, a pilot en route to Knoxville reported electrical problems on board his Cessna-172 before air traffic controllers lost contact. Emergency transmitter signals led rangers and the Civil Air Patrol to his crash site between Clingmans Dome and Collins Gap. The pilot did not survive.

On the A.T., follow beds of moss, ferns and wood sorrel to Mount Love (6,366 feet), the eastern shoulder of Clingmans Dome. There, on April 26, 1992, the high Smokies fatally caught another pilot off guard. Flying a Cessna-310 in inclement weather, a private pilot crashed into Mount Love. Over two days of navigating sheer cliffs in two feet of snow, rescuers found the pilot. Thick vegetation now covers the site. Continue south on the A.T., bordered with pink turtlehead, hobblebush, Clinton's lily and false hellebore, to the top of Clingmans Dome.

To hike this 7.5-mile section one-way, arrange a shuttle, or just walk the 3-mile round trip from Newfound Gap to Indian Gap. Most of the spring wildflowers are along this section. It also makes a great high-elevation, winter hike when the Clingmans Dome Road is closed from December to April. Frozen fog (rime ice) encases tree branches and other vegetation in artistic sculptures.

Appalachian Trail: Clingmans Dome to Silers Bald

Led by Harvey Broome, an attorney from Knoxville, and environmentalist Ernie Dickerman, conservationists gathered on Clingmans Dome in protest. In 1966, the GSMNP superintendent proposed a "Skyway Drive" from Clingmans Dome across the rugged crest of the Smokies to Deal's Gap at the western end of the park. Prime wilderness areas would be destroyed. "Save

Our Smokies" hike was organized. Hikers departed the Dome, followed the A.T. south to Buckeye Gap and descended along Miry Ridge Trail. After seventeen miles, they arrived in Elkmont. Six hundred supporters attended the rally; most completed a portion of the hike.

Hike this A.T. section in tribute to those who worked to preserve its wilderness beauty. Pass the sign reading, "A.T./Clingmans Dome Bypass Trail." In less than ½ mile, climb Mount Buckley (6,582 feet). Watch for Rugel colonies and other wildflowers. Some ancient Fraser firs, resistant to balsam woolly adelgids, are here. Endangered moss spiders stay hidden. At 2.7 miles, reach Goshen Prong Trail. It meanders along an old railroad grade to Elkmont (one-way, from Clingmans Dome to Elkmont: 13.9 miles). Cascading streams, seclusion, changing forest types, a small cave and railroad relics beckon hikers to follow this route. For those with backcountry camping permits, Camp #30 at Three Forks offers a historic, beautiful setting. Little River Logging Company's old camp rested between three churning streams, tumbling from the north flank of Clingmans Dome.

Back on the A.T., Double Springs Gap Shelter is located about half a mile farther. Each spring leaves its subterranean chamber to trickle down the spine of the Smokies into two separate states. Waters born to the earth only fifty yards apart will take separate river journeys before mingling in the Gulf of Mexico.

Myron Avery on the state line with a measuring wheel. *Courtesy of Albert "Dutch" Roth Collection, University of Tennessee–Knoxville Libraries.*

Mid-summer, look for large purple-fringed orchids and bluebead lilies. Rock outcroppings offer views of Clingmans Dome. Cross the "Narrows," barely wide enough for two feet side by side.

Five miles from Clingmans Dome, arrive at Silers Bald. A view of Clingmans Dome is often obscured by vegetation or low clouds. An abandoned copper mine is located on Silers. Others dot Hazel Creek in the valley below. A pilot was rescued below Silers Bald from a small plane crash in January 1978. A ten-mile roundtrip to Silers Bald makes a great day-trip destination for the avid hiker.

Trails along Clingmans Dome Road

Road Prong Trail

"Doubtful of a road ever crossing the Smokies," wrote historian John Preston Arthur in 1914. In his book, *Western North Carolina, A History (From 1730 to 1913)*, he continued, "During the Civil War, Col. Thomas...and Cherokee Indians...did make a so-called wagon road through this gap, now called Collins Gap; and through it in 1864, General Robert B. Vance carried a section of artillery, dragging the dismounted canon...over the bare stones...but no other vehicle has passed this frightful road...and it is even dangerous to walk over its precipitous and rock-ribbed course. No other road has ever been attempted, and this one has been abandoned, except by horsemen and footmen."

Mr. Arthur would have been amazed. Pushing all doubts aside, the CCC crossed the high Smokies in the 1930s with a new road through a new gap, called Newfound Gap, 1.2 miles from the old wagon road. At Indian Gap (5,272 feet, and no longer known as Collins Gap), the Road Prong Trail begins at a parking area north of Clingmans Dome Road.

In 1859, Professor Guyot described this route as a "difficult mule path," adding, "The top of these ridges are usually sharp and rocky, deeply indented and winding considerably, covered in dense growth...travel over them is extremely difficult and almost impractical. Neither the White Man nor the Indian hunter venture in the wilderness."

Venture. Be a "footman." Hike a bit of history, where Indians blazed a trail one hundred years ago and Civil War soldiers stumbled bearing heavy weapons. Follow the path of pigs that required a penny to cross the turnpike, while farmers paid six and a quarter cents apiece.

Time for reflection is a bonus. Few people take this rough, rocky route. But, natural rewards await: giant boulders, massive red spruce, churning-white streams, waterfalls and wildflowers. Several springs and tributaries gently flow into the main stream. Waters deepen, providing a perfect habitat for the native brook trout. Look for its orange belly. Red dots splatter its sides.

From Clingmans Dome Road to its exit at Newfound Gap Road, the Road Prong trail descends 1,672 feet in 3.3 miles. The A.T. intersects near Indian Gap. The popular Chimney Tops Trail joins at 2.4 miles.

Spruce-Fir Forest Nature Trail

See the Spruce-Fir Trail as an environmental classroom. Go elsewhere for great views and a lovely landscape. A quick glance and a narrow mind will miss the education this short trail has to offer. Spend some time on the half-mile loop trail with an ecologist's eye. How has life changed here since the Fraser firs died? What might benefit? Why are hardwoods growing in a conifer forest zone?

What would cause massive red spruce to uproot? Why does that yellow birch grow on stilts? What wildflowers bloom among the thick carpet of mosses and ferns?

Is anybody home? The red-cheeked salamander? A northern flying squirrel? A saw-whet owl? Whose midden pile is that? What is that songster? Is this its home, or is it just passing through?

Traveling 2.7 miles from Newfound Gap Road, stop at the small parking area south of the road. Mosey along the trail at a slow pace. Observe something about the spruce-fir forest ecosystem that you've never noticed before.

Sugarland Mountain Trail

Although the trail falls 3,500 feet from Clingmans Dome Road to Little River Road (across from Laurel Falls trailhead), the descent is gradual over the one-way, 12.3-mile route. On Clingmans Dome Road, park 3.5 miles from Newfound Gap Road at the Fork Ridge trailhead. Cross the highway. Hike a connector trail to the A.T. Leave the A.T. at 0.2 miles and pass Mt. Collins Shelter.

Sugarland Mountain Trail offers giant red spruce and yellow birch. Little effort and easy strides provide grand views of surrounding valleys, Mount

Spruce-Fir Nature Trail. *Illustration by Tim Worsham.*

Le Conte and Chimney Tops. The twin "chimneys" are actually part of Sugarland Mountain, but their trail access is on Newfound Gap Road. When fall leaves drop, look for Clingmans Dome Tower.

A narrow-ridge trail, huge boulders, changing forest types and a wide variety of wildflowers are extra perks. Rough Creek Trail to Elkmont and Huskey Gap Trails to Elkmont and Newfound Gap Road depart this trail along the way, suggesting alternate loops on another day.

Fork Ridge Trail

Back at your car on Clingmans Dome Road, Fork Ridge Trail (with its trailhead at 5,880 feet) leads five miles south to Deep Creek Trail. Continue ten miles downstream from the juncture to a campground near Bryson City, North Carolina, or either backtrack to the Dome Road or go left up Deep Creek Trail to Newfound Gap Road.

A virgin spruce forest, one of the few in the park that escaped the logger's saw, encloses Fork Ridge's upper trail near the Dome Road. Massive red spruce trees survive. Impressive yellow birches seek sunlight in opened areas. Pass through large beech and more birch before Fork Ridge enters a hemlock forest. Shh—silence, and not a care in the world. A hardwood forest and rhododendron tunnel usher you to Deep Creek.

If your day only allows for a short hike, consider an in-and-out walk for about a mile. Rock outcrops, pushed vertical by herculean forces during the mountain's birth, are sliced with lightning bolts of white quartz. Don't miss the northern flying squirrel nesting box high on the right. Find wildflowers, mountain laurel and rhododendron blooming in June.

In a letter dated March 6, 1937, the superintendent of the new GSMNP, J.R. Eakin, wrote, "Tsali is said to have hidden in a cave on the upper stretches of Deep Creek." That small cave, legend has it, is located near Keg Drive Branch off Fork Ridge Trail. Tsali, a Cherokee Indian leader, was fleeing U.S. soldiers during the forced removal of the Cherokees to lands in Oklahoma.

Fork Ridge Trail is part of North Carolina's Mountains-to-Sea Trail (MST), beginning at Clingmans Dome and ending at the Atlantic Ocean. Twenty-eight of its one thousand miles traverse GSMNP. From the Dome, MST follows the A.T. to Sugarland Mountain Trail and crosses the road at Fork Ridge.

Mountains-to-Sea Trail

Clingmans Dome, the highest point in GSMNP, on the Appalachian Trail, and in TN, is also the start of the Mountains-to-Sea Trail (MST). From here, you can walk 1000 miles across NC. In the Park, the MST goes up the Clingmans Dome paved path and joins the A.T. heading north. For 3.7 miles, the two trails traverse through Fraser fir and spruce in a hobbit-like setting. It takes you up Little Mt. Collins and Mt. Collins, two wooded tops that are not identified on the trail. Most A.T. and MST hikers just blow past them.

At the intersection with Sugarlands Mt. Trail, the MST says good-bye to the A.T., crosses Clingmans Dome Rd., and plunges down to Deep Creek. It eventually wiggles to it official end in the Park at Mingus Mill. MST follows the Blue Ridge Parkway for 300 miles until the BRP leaves NC. After walking past farms, through small towns and state parks, the trail terminates at Jockey's Ridge State Park in the Outer Banks.

However, don't think that the MST will be a downward slide to the Atlantic Ocean. As you stand on top of Old Smoky and look east, you won't be able to see the water. If you're lucky and the day is clear, Mt. Mitchell, the highest point east of the Mississippi, might be visible...

——Danny Bernstein, author of *The Mountains-to-Sea Trail Across North Carolina: Walking a Thousand Miles through Wilderness, Culture and History*

Danielle "Danny" Bernstein has hiked all nine hundred miles of GSMNP trails, the A.T. and the MST. A hiking leader for Carolina Mountain Club, Danny is also a prolific author on hiking and the outdoors.

Noland Divide Trail

In 11.6 miles, Noland Divide Trail, the steepest Park trail in North Carolina, drops 4,129 feet from Clingmans Dome Road (5,929 feet) to Deep Creek Campground (1,800). Hike this route through a wide variety of forest types in eight hours or so, or drive from here to Nova Scotia to see all the forest zones. Take your pick. The trailhead is found at an old gated roadway 5.5 miles from Newfound Gap Road.

Each forest community offers different types of trees, a varied range of flowers and special creatures that inhabit them. A huge stand of red spruce occupies the upper slopes. Within a mile of Clingmans Dome Road, the largest yellow birch tree in North Carolina grows near the trail. In summer, flame azalea, laurels and rhododendron bloom. Pink lady slippers bloom in pine forests, scorched by a severe fire in 2001. Rock outcroppings afford sweeping views. Pole Creek and Noland Creek Trails intersect before ending at Deep Creek Campground.

Clingmans Dome/Forney Ridge Parking Lot

In 1859, Arnold Guyot described the main Smokies ridgeline near Clingmans Dome, saying, "After a short turn to the west, it sends out a long, powerful ridge, called Forney Ridge to the southwest."

Forney Ridge and Welch Ridge frame the Forney Creek watershed. Once a thriving community, settlers farmed valley bottomland and grazed cattle on its high mountain balds. Andres Thompson grazed livestock on what is now known as Andrews Bald; the name, unfortunately, was misspelled years ago.

Most major valleys in the park—such as Cades Cove, Cataloochee and Greenbrier—are pierced by roads. Forney Creek valley, however, must be explored on foot. Clingmans Dome parking lot at its northern end is the closest road access. The southern end is approached by boat across Fontana Lake and by foot on trails from Hazel and Noland Creek areas.

From 1909 to the 1920s, Norwood Lumber Company logged Forney Creek Valley heavily. Railroads cut through forests. Incline railways inched even higher. Within a mile of Clingmans Dome, red spruce was removed. Piles of debris were discarded. Timber on steep mountain cliffs, inaccessible by train, was rolled, pulled or skidded to waiting rail cars, demolishing everything in its path.

Stand on overlooks along Newfound Gap Road on the North Carolina side of the park. See scars from old railroad lines, snaking up the rugged terrain. Look for "ballhooting" scars where heavy, gravity-powered tree trunks, thrust downhill, ripped weaker vegetation out by the roots. In 1925, sparks from a railroad ignited dry brush piles, setting the valley ablaze. Fire scars on trees are sad reminders.

Forney Ridge Trail

On May 22, 2012, a ribbon cutting ceremony celebrated the completion of a major campaign to rehabilitate the Forney Ridge Trail. After several years and thousands of man-hours breaking boulders, crushing stones, building steps, funneling water run-offs and carrying tons of rocks, the popular trail has been restored. Crew and volunteers shoveled six hundred thousand pounds of stone fill, moved four hundred thousand pounds of rock into place, fashioned eight hundred native stone steps and pavers and built 150 timber steps.

Forney Ridge Trail leads to Andrews Bald (5,680 feet), the highest, most easily reached grassy bald of the twenty found in GSMNP. Thousands of boot-treads, constant groundwater seepage, poor drainage and rutted ground surfaces made travel rough, messy and often dangerous. Hikers, trying to avoid deep pockets of standing water, widened trail areas and flattened precious vegetation. Over sixty stone water bars and seventy timber ones were constructed to divert the water across the trail and down the mountainside.

Andrews Bald is a gem. Only Gregory Bald near Cades Cove has a more spectacular flame azalea and Catawba rhododendron garden. Rhododendrons crown Andrews' highest region; azaleas adorn its southern edge. Andrews' western slope boasts a rare high-elevation bog. A carnivorous sundew, three species of orchids and a southern bog lemming live here. Near the trail's entrance onto Andrews Bald, don't miss wild lilies of the valley blooming in June. A Federal Species of Concern, the Smoky Mountain manna grass (*Glyceria nubigena*) grows on top.

Forney Ridge Trail ends at Springhouse Branch Trail at 4.5 miles. Perhaps you'll choose to just hike the 1.7 miles to Andrews Bald. Take a friend, a family and a picnic lunch. Take a heavy heart and come back renewed.

Clingmans Dome

Forney Creek Trail

The Forney Ridge Trail leaves Clingmans Dome parking lot, and 1.1 miles later, the Forney Creek Trail branches off to the right. Fontana Lake is 11.0 miles away. A strenuous, tough loop of Forney Creek and Forney Ridge Trails, with several risky river crossings, is over 15.0 miles long.

Three miles down Forney Creek Trail, find Rock Slab Falls, the park's longest water slide. (Caution: A three-mile descent becomes a hard, three-mile steady climb on the return.) The falls are actually two slides. Water leaves a chute through a pile of rocks before gliding smoothly down a 110-foot sandstone. Gray sandstone rocks are streaked with three-inch-wide quartz, like cream cheese oozing out of pressed bagels. The creek narrows and slides again, 135 feet to a shallow pool of water.

Railway and logging parts left by Norwood Lumber Company are scattered in the creek and along the trail. Part of a stone railroad trestle remains. Near the mid-point of the Forney Creek/Forney Ridge loop, Backcountry Camp #71 occupies the site of the Forney Creek CCC camp.

Listen. Which trail is offering you an invitation? A trail of beauty? A trail with a message? A path of history? Or perhaps one of adventure?

High vistas, mountain meadows, secluded firs, rocky landscapes, a forest in transition….what will you choose?

Catch Clingmans Dome early morning, late evening or even after dark, and you may have it to yourself. See a sunrise from the parking lot and a sunset from the tower. Clingmans Dome may be boldly visible or discreetly covered in mist. No matter. Silent and proud, Clingmans Dome has secrets to reveal. Will they be secrets of the mountain—or secrets lying dormant within you?

Without a sound, a man disappeared into the clouds, climbing to the top of Clingmans Dome, alone. The deck of the observation tower was empty on this cold, drizzly day. Without expression, he gazed into the gray as if looking hundreds of miles into the distance. After many moments, he murmured, "It was right to come." Quietly, he turned and descended the paved trail, presumably with a lighter load.

Hubert Bebb planned a tower accessible by those with physical limitations long before current standards were imposed. Dr. John Spencer, a hemiplegic, climbs the Dome in this July 2012 photograph. *Photo by the author.*

CHAPTER 11

ENJOYING THE VIEW

Visibility at Clingmans Dome was less than one hundred feet. Clouds engulfed trail, tree and tower. Family members arrived eager to continue their adventure. Activities in age-specific, Junior Ranger workbooks took child and parent on educational assignments throughout the Park. Upon completion, the new Junior Ranger would be "sworn in" and awarded a badge by a park ranger. By noon, two Junior Ranger wannabes came to the Dome.

Mom joined daughter, age nine, at the parking lot exhibit to find the facts she needed about high-elevation forests.

"It's not here," the girl said. "I'll go to the Visitor Center."

"What's your activity at Clingmans Dome, son?" asked Dad, invigorated after a tree hunt at Chimney Tops.

"He's supposed to climb to the top of Clingmans Dome and draw what he sees from the tower," Mom answered.

The five-year-old little boy looked innocently up into the cloud-choked trail: "I can leave it blank!"

Clingmans' mist often hides scenic views. On other days, the mountain's six thousand feet may lift viewers above the clouds—thick, white puffs filling lowland valleys like whipped cream on an ice cream sundae. Steamy summer haze can often blur distant views. Summer thunderstorms may envelope the Dome. But when the sky is blue and cirrus clouds wisp high overhead, the 360-degree view from Clingmans Dome Tower is magnificent.

CLINGMANS DOME

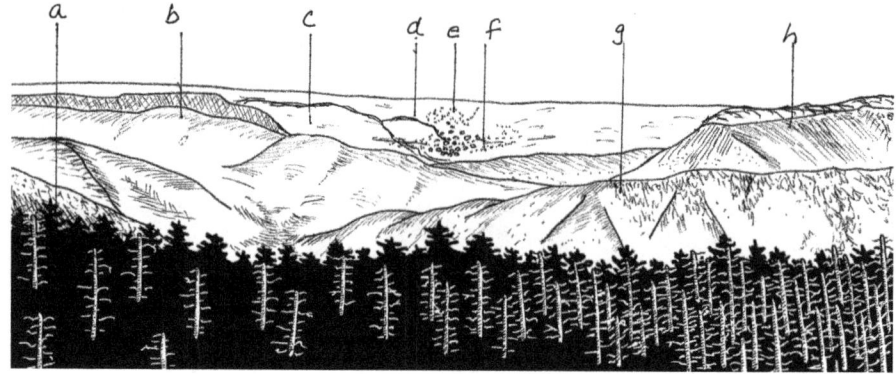

Northern view from Clingmans Dome Observation Platform. *Illustration by Tim Worsham.*

NORTHERN VIEW

A) MOUNT LOVE:
- 6,420 feet, 0.5 miles
- Named by Professor Guyot for Dr. Samuel Love, who helped measure Clingmans Dome.
- Fifth-highest peak in GSMNP.

B) BLANKET MOUNTAIN:
- 4,609 feet, 7.7 miles
- In 1802, while surveying the boundary between government and Indian lands, Return Jonathan Meigs tied a blanket to a tall tree to triangulate his position. Others claim that smoke signals, fanned with blankets by Indians, gave the peak its name.
- Located near Jakes Creek Trail in Elkmont; Campsite #27 is near the base.
- Logged by Little River Lumber Co. A railroad-ignited fire burned for months.
- A 1930s fire tower and cabin were removed. An old chimney and footers remain.

C) COVE MOUNTAIN:
- 4,077 feet, 11.0 miles
- Northern boundary of the park; Hike 2.7 miles beyond Laurel Falls.
- Eighty-foot fire tower; One of seven NP air quality monitoring stations.

Highest Mountain in the Great Smokies

d) **Bluff Mountain:**
   - 3,069 feet, 20.0 miles
   - 35.0 miles east of Knoxville, Tennessee
   - Site of a popular hotel in the 1920s; now mountain-top development, recreation, lodging.

e) **Pigeon Forge, Tennessee:**
   - 1,010 feet, 15.0 miles

f) **Gatlinburg, Tennessee:**
   - 1,289 feet, 10.5 miles
   - North entrance to GSMNP, Sugarlands Visitor Center and Park Headquarters.
   - Access to Roaring Fork and Cherokee Orchard Roads, GSMNP; Uplands Field Research Lab is here.

g) **Sugarland Mountain:**
   - 5,494 feet, 5.0 miles
   - Long ridge parallel to Mount Le Conte; perpendicular to GSM ridgeline. Twelve-mile trail from Dome Road to Little River Road.
   - Mount Collins (6,188 feet), 0.5 miles south, is named for Robert Collins, who led Professor Guyot to measure Smoky peaks.
   - Excellent views of Mount Le Conte and Blanket Mountain. Chimney Tops rises from Sugarland Mountain.
   - Two major watersheds: West-flank waters flow toward Elkmont. Eastside waters flow northward through Gatlinburg and Pigeon Forge.

h) **Mount Le Conte:**
   - 6,593 feet, 6.5 miles
   - Rises above Gatlinburg; Third-highest peak in GSMNP; A one-mile rise in four miles makes Le Conte the highest, steepest slope in eastern America.
   - Lies perpendicular to the main Smoky ridgeline; Joins the crest at Mount Kephart, 2.7 miles north on the A.T. from Newfound Gap.
   - Four major peaks: 1) Myrtle Point (view sunrise) 2) High Top (highest point) 3) Cliff Top (sunset view of Clingmans Dome) 4) West Point (previously Balsam Point).
   - Height accurately measured by Guyot. Named by Samuel Buckley for Professor John Le Conte for his help in 1858 to measure Clingmans Dome.
   - Mount Le Conte Lodge: Highest hike-in-only lodge in eastern United States. Llamas deliver supplies. Began in 1920s as a tent camp for politicians considering a new national park.
   - Roaring Fork creek flows a mile down Mount Le Conte; Grotto and Rainbow Falls drop off its side.

CLINGMANS DOME

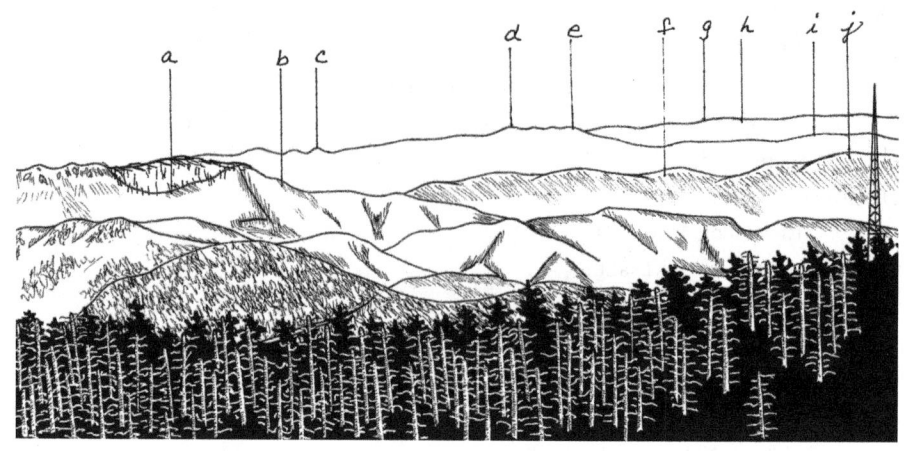

Eastern view from Clingmans Dome Observation Platform. *Illustration by Tim Worsham.*

EASTERN VIEW

A) **MOUNT LE CONTE:** *See Northern View*
B) **NEWFOUND GAP:**
- 5,046 feet, 5.5 miles
- Near junction of Newfound Gap Road and Clingmans Dome Road. On the North Carolina–Tennessee state line.
- Newfound Gap and Clingmans Dome are the best places in GSMNP to access the 2,100-mile A.T. A sign reads: "Mt. Katahdin, Maine: 1,972 miles." This A.T. section, built in 1932, was the first park project created for public use.
- Named for the "new" gap that was "found" through the Smokies to build a road.
- Civilian Conservation Corps (CCC) built parking lot, overlooks and rock walls in the 1930s. FDR dedicated the new GSMNP here on September 2, 1940.

C) **MOUNT GUYOT:**
- 6,621 feet, 17.0 miles
- Second-highest peak in the park.
- Named by Samuel Buckley for Arnold Guyot: commissioned in 1859, by Thomas Clingman, to re-measure "Smoky Dome" with more sophisticated instruments.

- Located north of Tricorner Knob, where the Balsam Mountain cross-range meets the main GSM ridgeline. The A.T. veers around its base. An unmaintained bushwhack leads to the top. Ramsey Cascades drops from its western slope.
- Surveyor's wooden tower from the 1920s has been removed.

D) BIG CATALOOCHEE MOUNTAIN:
- 6,155 feet, 20.0 miles
- Part of the Balsam Range; rises above Cataloochee Valley, North Carolina; elk reintroduced here in 2001 (25 elk) and 2002 (27 elk); In 2012, there was a healthy, growing elk population of 140.
- "Cataloochee" comes from a Cherokee Indian word that means "fringe standing erect," describing tall trees defining a ridgeline.
- An Indian path, known as "Cataloochee Trail," entered the valley's rich hunting grounds. In 1791, Cherokee Indians relinquished the area to white settlers. In the 1920–'30s, the NPS claimed ownership.
- Cataloochee Divide, the NP's southeastern boundary, also frames Cataloochee Valley. Here, Purchase Knob, a mountain donated to GSMNP, became home to the Appalachian Highlands Science Learning Center in 2001 to promote scientific research and education.

E) MOUNT MITCHELL:
- 6,684 feet, 73.0 miles
- Highest mountain in eastern America. It is named for Elisha Mitchell, who explored the area.
- Location: Black Mountain Range of Southern Appalachians; Blue Ridge Parkway milepost #355.4; 32 miles northeast of Asheville; a North Carolina State Park, surrounded by Pisgah National Forest; nearby: 1) Clingmans Peak (6,520 feet), named for Senator Clingman 2) Mount Craig, formerly Mount Guyot (6,647 feet), second-highest mountain in the East (Clingmans Dome, at 6,643 feet, is the third-highest).

F) NEWTON BALD:
- 5,000 feet, 8.0 miles
- In the pre-park era, the Newton family lived nearby.
- Newton Bald Trail leaves Smokemont Campground, ending 5.3 miles later at Thomas Divide Trail. Backcountry Camp # 52 is near its base.

G) MOUNT PISGAH:
- 5,721 feet, 43.0 miles
- Purchased in 1840 by Thomas Clingman; impoverished, he sold it in 1892 for $800.
- Sold to George Vanderbilt, who spent his fortune building Biltmore House in Asheville, North Carolina, the largest home in America. After 1914, his

widow sold 86,000 acres, including Mount Pisgah, to the U.S. government for $5.00 per acre to become Pisgah National Forest (first national forest in the East).
- Located twenty-two miles south of Asheville on the Blue Ridge Parkway, Milepost # 407. Site of Vanderbilt's Buck Springs Hunting Lodge; 1.7-mile trail to summit with 360-degree view and transmitter tower.

H) COLD MOUNTAIN:
- 6,030 feet, 38.0 miles
- Owned by George Vanderbilt; now part of Shining Rock Wilderness of Pisgah National Forest; located at Blue Ridge Parkway Milepost # 412; trails lead to summit.
- Made famous in novel *Cold Mountain*, by Charles Frazier, in 1997, as well as the 2003 movie of the same name.

I) CHEROKEE, NORTH CAROLINA (BEHIND RIDGE):
- 1,991 feet, 11.5 miles
- Qualla Cherokee Indian Boundary: ancestral home of Cherokee people.
- Artifacts date back more than 8,000 years; plants and animals of the Smokies provided food, medicine, clothing, tools and shelter. An eternal flame was sacred. So were their lands, the mountains and wildlife.
- In 1838, the U.S. government forced removal of the Eastern Cherokee to Oklahoma. Today, the sovereign nation of the Eastern Band of Cherokee borders the southern entrance to GSMNP. Cherokee people who returned, or descendants of those who either hid or kept their land, proudly preserve their culture.
- Cherokee Cultural District: Museum of the Cherokee Indian; Oconaluftee Indian Village; historical drama, *Unto These Hills*; authentic Indian arts and crafts.
- GSMNP's Oconaluftee Visitor Center and Museum are located inside the southern entrance. The word, "Oconaluftee," comes from an old Cherokee village with that name. It means "by the river."

J) THOMAS RIDGE:
- 4,600 feet, 8.0 miles
- Named for Colonel William Thomas, a white man who befriended Cherokee Indians, became their chief in 1839, built the road over Indian Gap, commanded Confederate Indian troops in the Civil War and bought land for the Cherokee that became part of the Qualla Boundary.
- Driving from Cherokee, Newfound Gap Road leaves the Oconaluftee River to climb up and along the crest of Thomas Ridge.

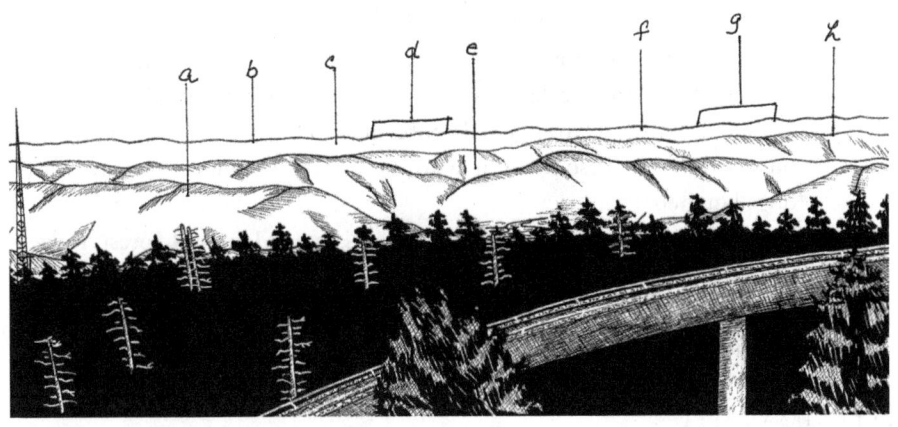

Southern view from Clingmans Dome Observation Platform. *Illustration by Tim Worsham.*

Southern View

A) ANDREWS BALD:
- 5,920 feet, 1.5 miles
- A double-peak on Forney Ridge; owned by Champion Fibre but never logged.
- A popular hike, 1.7 miles from Clingmans Dome Parking Lot; flame azaleas; rare flowers; rare southern mountain bog; highest bald in GSMNP.
- Corrupted name of Andres Thompson, who grazed livestock there.

B) FRY MOUNTAIN:
- 4,502 feet, 14.0 miles
- In Swain County, near Bryson City, North Carolina.
- Fire tower removed in 2006.

C) STANDING INDIAN MOUNTAIN:
- 5,499 feet, 37.0 miles
- Outside GSMMP in Nantahala National Forest; highest point in Macon County, North Carolina.
- Its Cherokee Indian name means: "where the man stood." Legend says that an Indian warrior, assigned to guard the summit, watched for a winged monster stealing Cherokee children. He fled and turned to stone. Lightning sent by the Great White Spirit killed the monster.

D) NANTAHALA NATIONAL FOREST:
- One of three national forests that borders GSMNP; largest of four National Forests in North Carolina.

- Name is a Cherokee word meaning: "Land of the Noonday Sun," because steep mountain cliffs only allow sunlight to reach the valley by midday. Three ranger districts have Cherokee names: Nantahala District, Franklin, North Carolina; Cheoah, at Robbinsville, North Carolina, means "otter"; Tusquitee, at Murphy, North Carolina: "where water dogs laughed."
- Noted features: Nantahala Gorge, Joyce-Kilmer Memorial Forest, rugged wilderness, numerous streams. Nikwasi Mound in Franklin: spiritual center of ancient Cherokee village.
- Bartram, Foothills and Mountain-to-Sea Trails cross this region. A.T. follows the crest of the Nantahala Mountains.

E) FONTANA LAKE:
- 1,709 feet, 8.5 miles
- GSMNP's southern boundary; Graham County, North Carolina; see GSM and Clingmans Dome by boat. About 90 percent is owned by NPS and NFS.
- At 480 feet, it is the highest dam in eastern America and fourth-highest in the United States; built 1942–1945, impounding the Little Tennessee River to generate electricity to manufacture supplies for World War II for the aluminum plant (ALCOA) and the weapons lab in Oak Ridge, Tennessee. Displaced six hundred families; flooded villages and old logging towns.
- Receives waters from Clingmans Dome streams, as well as Nantahala, Tuckasegee and Oconaluftee Rivers. Three narrow lakes, downstream from Fontana Dam, also border GSMNP: Cheoah, Calderwood and Chilhowee.
- Depth: average 130 feet; Water: more than 10,000 acres; Shoreline: 240 miles; Dam: more than 2,000 feet wide; Flood control: water level fluctuates about 56 feet each year in annual drawdown by the Tennessee Valley Authority.
- Northbound A.T. hikers cross Fontana Dam before entering GSMNP. Some trails to Smokies accessed by boat. Deep, cold waters offer great fishing.
- Movies filmed here: 1) *Nell* (1994), starring Jodie Foster 2) *The Fugitive* (1994), starring Harrison Ford. The old dam on Cheoah Lake was site of the "dam jump." Dillsboro, North Carolina, was the site of the famous train wreck.
- A 1940s town was created for six thousand dam workers. It is now Fontana Village (in Italian, *Fontana* means "fountain").

Highest Mountain in the Great Smokies

F) CHEOAH BALD: *See Western View*
G) SNOWBIRD MOUNTAINS:
- 30.0 miles
- Outside GSMNP; in Graham County, North Carolina, near Robbinsville, North Carolina: grave site of Chief Junaluska's, who saved Andrew Jackson's life in War of 1812 but was forced west on the Trail of Tears in 1838. He returned to Robbinsville, where the United States granted him citizenship and his own land.
- The thirty-six-mile Cherohala Skyway crosses the region. The name joins "Cherokee" and "Nantahala," the two national forests through which it passes. Poles were erected here to allow northern flying squirrels to safely cross the highway. Nearby is "Tail of the Dragon," eleven miles of roadway that twists into 318 curves, a motorcyclist's heaven. A section of "the Dragon" borders the southwestern corner of GSMNP.
- Lake Santeelah, Joyce-Kilmer Memorial Forest and historic Snowbird Mountain Lodge are here.

H) HIGH ROCKS: *See Western View*

Western view from Clingmans Dome Observation Platform. *Illustration by Tim Worsham.*

Western View

a) CHEOAH BALD:
- 5,062 feet, 19.0 miles
- Outside GSMNP; in Nantahala National Forest; Nantahala River Gorge at southeastern base.
- Probable site where botanist William Bartram began his 1770s journey through Southern Appalachia. The 115-mile Bartram Trail through Georgia and North Carolina begins at Cheoah.
- "Cheoah," with its numerous streams, takes the Cherokee word for "otter." Endemic Cheoah salamander lives here. Blue Nantahala slate forms knife-edge formation south of summit.
- A.T. crosses Cheoah, dubbed the worst "gut-buster" climb or "knee-buster" descent on the A.T. From Cheoah Bald to Clingmans Dome via the A.T. is approximately fifty-five miles.

b) SNOWBIRD MOUNTAINS: *See Southern View*

c) HIGH ROCKS:
- 5,188 feet, 8.2 miles
- On Welch Ridge, a long ridge that leaves the Smokies ridgeline at Silers Bald, 4.9 A.T.-miles south of Clingmans Dome; separates Hazel and Forney Creeks.
- In the early 1900s, Norwood Lumber Company logged the Forney Creek area while Ritter Co. logged Hazel.
- A fire tower was removed in the 1980s, but the foundation and a clay-chinked, chestnut cabin (with cistern) remain; brown bats occupy the attic.
- Composed of Thunderhead sandstone with white quartz veins and pebbly conglomerates.

d) SHUCKSTACK MOUNTAIN:
- 4,020 feet, 18.0 miles
- Above Fontana Lake at southern Park boundary. To some, its shape resembles bunched corn stalks.
- One of three remaining fire towers in GSMNP that visitors can climb (others are Mount Cammerer and Mount Sterling). Cross Fontana Dam, climb steeply 3.4 miles on the A.T. to the ridgeline, where a 0.1-mile spur trail leads to the tower, old chimney and cistern.
- Views of the GSMs to the north and east; Unicoi Mountains, west; Snowbird and Nantahala Mountains, south; and Fontana Lake below. See Clingmans Dome on a clear day.
- Fire lookout until 1950–'60s; tower operators had commanding views of 1940s dam construction.

Highest Mountain in the Great Smokies

E) MOUNT BUCKLEY:
- 6,580 feet, 0.5 miles
- Named by Professor Guyot for Samuel Buckley, who joined Clingman's 1858 expedition.
- Fourth-highest peak in GSMNP.
- Rare moss spiders, Rugel's Indian plantain and virgin Fraser firs that resisted the adelgids are found here.

F) NORTH CAROLINA–TENNESSEE STATE LINE

G) GREGORY BALD:
- 4,949 feet, 21.0 miles
- Above Cades Cove, southwestern corner of Park.
- Flame azalea gardens, blooming June–July; two trail routes.
- Named for Russell Gregory (1795–1864), who lived on Gregory in the 1820s. He (and others) purchased it in 1853. He grazed livestock there and was killed by Confederate soldiers.
- The original A.T. crossed Gregory Bald but was rerouted in 1948 after Fontana Dam was built.
- Cherokee believed the chief of their rabbit clan lived on this mountain. The Cherokee name meant "Rabbit Place."

H) THUNDERHEAD MOUNTAIN:
- 5,527 feet, 12.0 miles
- On the backbone of the Smokies, nearly 15 A.T.-miles south of Clingmans Dome; Highest mountain in western GSMNP, rising 3,000 feet from its base.
- Named by settlers for severe summer thunderstorms common in the high Smokies; listed as "Thunderhead" on Guyot's 1859 survey; Cherokee word meant: "oak gall place"; Thunderhead sandstone was named after this peak.
- Three distinct peaks: the lowest, <u>Rocky Top</u> (5,440 feet), provides 360-degree views and was made famous in a 1967 song written in Gatlinburg. University of Tennessee (UT) football games adopted it. NFL player Peyton Manning and his UT coach posed for a poster photo op on Rocky Top.

I) CADES COVE (BEHIND RIDGE):
- 1,716 feet, 18.0 miles
- Historic buildings preserve the Park's cultural history; an eleven-mile roadway loops through a beautiful valley surrounded by the Smoky Mountains. Great wildlife viewing. Movie *The Doll Maker* (1984), starring Jane Fonda, was filmed here.

- Cherokee Indians hunted the valley before white settlers arrived in early 1830s.
- Clingmans Dome to Cades Cove:

By road: approximately 52 miles (1 hr. 30 mins.)

By foot: 23 miles—17 miles on the A.T. over Mount Buckley, Silers Bald, Thunderhead and Rocky Top; descend Bote Mountain Trail to either Anthony Creek or Russell Field Trails, and arrive at Cades Cove.

J) BLANKET MOUNTAIN: *See Northern View*

K) COVE MOUNTAIN: *See Northern View*

APPENDIX

CHECKLIST OF PLANTS AND ANIMALS REFERENCED IN TEXT

Mammals

American black bear (*Ursus americanus*)
Appalachian cottontail (*Sylvilagus obscurus*)
big brown bat (*Eptesicus fuscus*)
bobcat (*Lynx rufus*)
Carolina northern flying squirrel (*Glaucomys sabrinus coloratus*)
coyote (*Canis latrans*)
deer mouse (*Peromyscus maniculatus*)
eastern chipmunk (*Tamias striatus*)
eastern cottontail (*Sylvilagus floridanus*)
eastern gray squirrel (*Sciurus carolinensis*)
eastern small-footed bat (*Myotis leibii*)
European wild boar (*Sus scrofa*)
Indiana bat (*Myotis sodalis*)
little brown bat (*Myotis lucifugus*)
long-tailed shrew (*Sorex dispar*)
long-tailed weasel (*Mustela frenata*)
masked shrew (*Sorex cinereus*)
raccoon (*Procyon lotor*)
red fox (*Vulpes vulpes*)
red squirrel (*Tamiasciurus hudsonicus*)

rock vole (*Microtus chrotorrhinus*)
silver-haired bat (*Lasionycteris noctivagans*)
smoky shrew (*Sorex fumeus*)
southern bog lemming (*Synaptomys cooperi*)
southern flying squirrel (*Glaucomys volans*)
southern red-backed vole (*Clethrionomys gapperi*)
striped skunk (*Mephitis mephitis*)
Virginia opossum (*Didelphis virginiana*)
white-tailed deer (*Odocoileus virginianus*)

Spiders

spruce-fir moss spider (*Microhexura montivaga*)

Salamanders

imitator salamander (*Desmognathus imitator*)
pygmy salamander (*Desmognathus wrighti*)
red-cheeked, or Jordan's salamander (*Plethodon jordani*)

Snakes

black rat snake (*Elaphe [Pantherophis] obsoleta*)
timber rattlesnake (*Crotalus horridus*)

Birds

American robin (*Turdus migratorius*)
Blackburnian warbler (*Setophaga fusca*)
black-capped chickadee (*Poecile atricapillus*)
black-throated blue warbler (*Setophaga caerulescens*)

APPENDIX

black-throated green warbler (*Setophaga virens*)
blue-headed vireo (*Vireo solitarius*)
brown creeper (*Certhia americana*)
Canada warbler (*Wilsonia canadensis*)
cedar waxwing (*Bombycilla cedrorum*)
chestnut-sided warbler (*Setophaga pensylvanica*)
common raven (*Corvus corax*)
dark-eyed junco (*Junco hyemalis*)
eastern towhee (*Pipilo erythrophthalmus*)
golden-crowned kinglet (*Regulus satrapa*)
gray catbird (*Dumetella carolinensis*)
hairy woodpecker (*Picoides villosus*)
northern saw-whet owl (*Aegolius acadicus*)
olive-sided flycatcher (*Contopus cooperi*)
pine siskin (*Carduelis pinus*)
red-breasted nuthatch (*Sitta canadensis*)
red crossbill (*Loxia curvirostra*)
ruby-throated hummingbird (*Archilochus colubris*)
ruffed grouse (*Bonasa umbellus*)
veery (*Catharus fuscescens*)
white pelican (*Pelecanus erythrorhynchos*)
winter wren (*Troglodytes hiemalis*)

Lichens

old man's beard *(genus: Usnea)*

Ferns

intermediate wood fern (*Dryopteris intermedia*)
mountain wood fern (*Dryopteris campyloptera*)
southern lady fern (*Athyrium filix-femina var. asplenioides*)

Appendix

Trees and Shrubs

Catawba rhododendron (*Rhododendron catawbiense*)
fire, or pin, cherry (*Prunus pensylvanica*)
flame azalea (*Rhododendron calendulaceum*)
Fraser fir (*Abies fraseri*)
mountain ash (*Sorbus americana*)
mountain maple (*Acer spicatum*)
red spruce (*Picea rubens*)
yellow birch (*Betula alleghaniensis*)

BIBLIOGRAPHY

Adams, Jonathan. "North America During the last 150,000 Years." Oak Ridge National Lab, TN. www.esd.ornl.gov/projects/qen/nercNORTHAMERICA.htm.

Allaback, Sarah. *Mission 66 Visitor Centers, a History of a Building Type.* U.S. Department of the Interior, National Park Service. http://www.cr.nps.gov/history/online_books/allaback/index.htm2000.

Alsop, Fred J., III. *Birds of the Smokies.* Gatlinburg, TN: GSMA, 2003.

Antonelli, Arthur. "Balsam Woolly Adelgid: A Pest of True Fir Species." *Extension Bulletin 1456.* Washington State University Cooperative Extension and USDA. Revised Feb. 1992.

Arbogast, Brian S., and Katelyn I. Schumacher. "Conservation Genetics of the Northern Flying Squirrel *(Glaucomys sabrinus coloratus)* in NC and Virginia." *Landscape and Conservation Genetics of the Northern Flying Squirrel.* Annual Performance Report, July 2009–June 2010. Wildlife Diversity Program, NCWRC, Raleigh, NC.

Arthur, F.H., and F.P. Hain. "Seasonal History of the Balsam Woolly Adelgid (Homoptera: Adelgidae) in Natural Stands and Plantations of Fraser Firs." *Journal of Economic Entomology* 77, no. 5 (May 1984): 1154–58.

Arthur, John Preston. *WNC, a History, from 1730 to 1913.* Raleigh, NC: Edwards and Broughton Printing Co., 1914.

Bebb, Ellen. Phone conversation. October 10, 2012.

BIBLIOGRAPHY

Bebb, Hubert. February 27, 1959 letter from Bebb and Olson, Architects to Board of Trustees at *National Park Magazine* regarding Clingmans Dome Observation Tower. GSMNP Archives.

Bell, C. Ritchie, and Anne H. Lindsey. *Fall Color and Woodland Harvests.* Chapel Hill, NC: Laurel Hill Press, 1990.

Bernstein, Danny. "Bernard Elias." *Carolina Mountain Club e-Newsletter*, October 26, 2005.

Bird, Claire, and Coleman McCleneghan. "Morphological and Functional Diversity of Ectomycorrhizal Fungi on Roan Mountain (NC/TN)." *Southeastern Naturalist* 4, no. 1 (2005): 121–32.

Blackmun Ora. *WNC, Its Mountains, and Its People to 1880.* Boone, NC: Appalachian Consortium Press, 1980.

Blanton, Jack. "Rain Greets Opening of Park Tower." *Knoxville Journal* 24, October 1959.

Boynton, Allen. Updated by Chris Kelly. "Carolina Northern Flying Squirrel." *Wildlife Profile* NCWRC, Raleigh, NC: Division of Conservation Education, Updated 2007.

Brewer, Carson. "Clingmans Dome Tower Opened: Chill/Drizzle Mars Ceremonies." *Knoxville News-Sentinel*, October 24, 1959.

———. "Clingmans Dome Tower Opens New Scenes to Park Visitors." *Knoxville News-Sentinel*, October 25, 1959.

———. *Hiking in the Great Smokies.* Knoxville: self-published, 1986.

———. "How High Is Mt. Craig?" *Knoxville News-Sentinel*, April 4, 1976.

Brill, David. "The Nation's Best-loved Park, at 75." *Smokies Life* 2, no. 2.

Brodo, Irwin M., Sylvia Duran Sharnoff and Stephen Sharnoff. *Lichens of North America.* New Haven, CT: Yale University Press, 2007.

Brooks, Maurice. *The Appalachians.* Boston: Houghton Mifflin Co., 1965.

Broome, Harvey. *Out Under the Sky in the Great Smokies.* Knoxville: University of Tennessee Press, 2001.

Brown, Gary. *The Bear Almanac: A Comprehensive Guide to the Bears of the World*, 2nd Ed. Guilford, CT: The Lyons Press, 2009.

Brown, Margaret Lynn. *The Wild East: A Biography of the Great Smoky Mountains.* Gainesville: University Press of Florida, 2000.

"Buckley, Samuel Botsford," in *Handbook of Texas Online.* TX State Historical Association. http://www.tshaonline.org/handbook/online/articles/fbu07.

Buckley, Samuel Botsford. "Mountains of North Carolina and Tennessee." *American Journal of Science and Arts* XXVII, March 1859.

Burkhart, Heather (great-granddaughter of Hubert Bebb). Phone conversation. December 8, 2012.

Bibliography

Burns, Inez. "The Civilian Conservation Corps in TN." *Smoky Mountain Historical Society Journal* XXIV, no. 3. Autumn 1998.

Campbell, Carlos. *Birth of a National Park.* Knoxville: University of Tennessee Press, 1993.

———. February 25, 1959 letter from Great Smoky Mountain Conservation Association to Mr. Conrad Wirth, Director of NPS. GSMNP Archives.

———. Interview with Susan Bratton, park biologist. "History of Grassy Balds of GSMNP," May 22, 1975. Print.

Carr, Ethan. *Mission 66: Modernism and the National Park Dilemma.* Amherst: University of Massachusetts Press, 2007.

Casada, Jim. "Streams of the Smokies: Forney Creek, Part 1." *Smoky Mountain Times.* www.thesmokymountaintimes.com/articles/2008/07/17/sports.

Chappelka, A.H., H.S. Neufeld, A.W. Davison, G.L. Somers and J.R. Renfro. "Ozone Injury on Cutleaf Coneflower (*Rudbeckia laciniata*) and crown-beard (*Verbesina occidentalis*) in GSMNP." *Environmental Pollution* 125 (2003), 53–59.

"Clingmans Dome Is Highest Peak in Great Smokies Park." *Asheville Citizen-Times,* August 7, 1951.

"Clingman's Dome Tower Dedicated." *Asheville Citizen,* October 24, 1959.

"Clingmans Dome Tower Is Symmetrical Beauty." *Asheville Citizen-Times,* May 22 1960.

Clingman, Thomas Lanier. "Mount Pisgah, North Carolina." *Appleton's Journal* 10, no. 249 (December 27, 1873): 817.

———. "North Carolina—Her Wealth, Resources, and History." *Appleton Journal* 5, no. 112 (1871): 587–88.

———. *Selections from the Speeches and Writings of Hon. Thomas L. Clingman of North Carolina: with Additions and Explanatory Notes.* Raleigh, NC: John Nichols Book and Job Printer, 1878.

Coggins, Allen R. *Place Names of the Smokies.* Gatlinburg, GA: GSMA, 1999.

Coleman, J.S., Jr. "Learn Much in Initial Hike to Clingmans." *Asheville Times,* July 5, 1929.

Community Tectonics Architects (now Red Chair Architects). "Hubert Bebb." www.redchairarchitects.com.

"Conference Abstracts: Host Resistance Studies to the Balsam Woolly Adelgid and Hemlock Woolly Adelgid." Alliance for Saving Threatened Forest. June 25, 2010. www.threatenedforests.com/research/conference-abstracts-balsam-woolly-adelgid-studies-with-fraser-firs.

"Couple Wed atop Tower on Clingman's Dome for 'Here's Where We Decided to Get Married.'" Newspaper article on file at GSMNP Archives, circa 1930s.

BIBLIOGRAPHY

Crisp, Lawrence. Interviewed by Mary Lindsay. January 28, 1976. Bryson City, North Carolina. "Transcript of Interview: History of Grassy Balds, GSMNP." www.nps.gov/history/history/online_books/grsm/4/interview14.htm.

Dana, James D. "Memoir of Arnold Guyot: 1807–1884." Read before the National Academy on April 21, 1886.

DeAngelo, Laura (lead author), and Brian Black (topic editor). "London Smog Disaster, England." In *Encyclopedia of Earth*. Edited by Cutler J. Cleveland. Washington, DC: Environmental Information Coalition, National Council for Science and the Environment. First published February 8, 2008. Revised July 3, 2012.

DeLozier, Kim. "Bears, Boars, and Bulls in GSMNP." Presentation at Wildlife Wilderness Week, Pigeon Forge, Tennessee. January 2012.

———. Keynote speaker. Bear presentation at fundraiser dinner for Appalachian Bear Rescue. Townsend, Tennessee. November 2011.

Dorr, Laurence J. "That Land of flowers, Swamps, and Alligators." S.B. Buckley's 1843 trip up the St. Johns River, Florida." *Brittonia* 44, no. 1 (January–March 1992): 1–13.

Dourson, Dan and Judy. "Land Snails of the Great Smoky Mountains (Eastern Region)." Unpublished manual for Appalachian Highlands Science Learning Center, Purchase Knob, GSMNP. In cooperation with ATBI/Discover Life in America project, July 2006.

Dykeman, Wilma. *At Home in the Smokies, a History Handbook for the GSMNP* (revised edition of Dykeman's *Highland Homeland, the People of the GRSMNP*). Washington, D.C.: NPS Publications, 1978.

Early, Chris G. *Warblers of the Great Lakes Region and Eastern North America*. Buffalo, NY: Firefly Books, 2003.

Ellison, George. "Buckley's Mountain." *Smoky Mountain News*, June 11, 2008.

———. "Guyot's Smokies." *Smoky Mountain News*, April 18, 2007.

———. *High Vistas: An Anthology of Nature Writing from WNC and the Great Smoky Mountains, Vol. I 1674–1900*. Charleston: The History Press, 2008.

———. "The Smells of Autumn." *Smoky Mountain News*, October 13, 2010.

Elpel, Thomas J. *Botany in a Day, the Patterns Method of Plant Identification*, 5th edition. Pony, MT: HOPS Press, LLC, 2008.

Fink, Paul. *Backpacking Was the Only Way*. Johnson City: East Tennessee State University, 1975.

Forbush, Edward Howe, and John Bichard May. *A Natural History of American Birds of Eastern and Central North America*. New York: Bramhall House, 1955.

Ford, Barbara. *Black Bear, the Spirit of the Wilderness.* Boston: Houghton-Mifflin, 1981.
Friddell, John. "Endangered and Threatened Wildlife and Plants; Designation of Critical Habitat for the Spruce-fir Moss Spider." *Federal Register* 66, no. 130. Department of the Interior, USFWS.
Frome, Michael. *Strangers in High Places.* Knoxville: University of Tennessee Press, 1980.
Garber, Anne. "Bebb's Legacy." *Mountain Press.* Date unknown.
George, Jean Craighead. *The Moon of the Chickarees.* New York: HarperCollins Publishers, 1992.
Gove, Doris. *Great Smoky Mountains Trivia.* Helena, MT: Riverbend Publishing, 2010.
Great Smoky Mountains Association blog. "Clingmans Dome." October 2011. www.smokiesinformation.org/blog.
"Great Smoky Mountains Explorers." *Asheville Citizen Times*, April 5 1931.
Great Smoky Mountains National Park. "Dispatches from the Field." www.nps.gov/grsm/naturescience/dispatches-main.htm.
———. "Science and Resource Pocket Guide." NPS, 2011.
Grimm, Candace. "Crash of Single Engine Plane in GSMNP." www.awalkinthewoods.com.
Gupton, Oscar, and Fred C. Swope. *Fall Wildflowers of the Blue Ridge and Great Smoky Mountains.* Charlottesville: University Press of Virginia, 1987.
Guyot, Arnold. "Measurement of the Mountains of Western North Carolina." *Asheville News*, July 8, 1860.
———. "Memoirs of Louis Agassiz: 1807–1873." Read before National Academy, April 1878.
———. "Notes on the Geography of the Mountain District of Western North Carolina." February 22, 1863, forwarded to offices of Coast and Geodetic Survey. Re-discovered 1929 by Myron Avery and Kenneth S. Boardman: published in *NC Historical Review* 15, July 1938.
Hairr, John. *North Carolina Rivers, Facts, Legends, and Lore.* Charleston, SC: The History Press, 2007.
Harp, Joel, and John Fridell. "Recovery Plan for the Spruce-fir Moss Spider (*Microhexura montivaga*)." Atlanta, GA: USFWS, Southeast Division, September 11, 1998.
Hayes, Matthew, Aaron Moody, Peter S. White, and Jennifer L. Costanza. "The influence of logging and Topography on the distribution of spruce-fir forests near their Southern limits in GSMNP, USA." *Plant Ecology.* Springer Science + Business Media. May 17, 2006.

Hendershot, Don. "EPA Director Says Balance Must be Struck in Creating Clean Air Plans." *Smoky Mountain News*, July 3, 2002.

Hollingsworth, Robert G., and Fred Hain. "Balsam Woolly Adelgid (Homoptera: Adelgidae) and Spruce-fir Decline in Southern Appalachians: Assessing Pest Relevance in a Damaged Ecosystem." *Florida Entomologist* 74, no. 2 (June 1991).

———. "Balsam Woolly Adelgid (Homoptera: Adelgidae) Effects on Wood and Bark Structure of Fraser Fir and Silver Fir." *Entomological Society of America.* 1992.

Hooks, Bill. *Whistle over the Mountain: Steam Logging in the Smokies.* (DVD produced by Jim Thurston), 2007.

Horn, Dennis, and Tavia Cathart. *Wildflowers of TN and the Ohio Valley and the Southern Appalachians.* Auburn, WA: Lone Pine Publishing and the Tennessee Native Plant Society, 2005.

Houk, Rose. *Frequently Asked Questions about Bats.* Tucson: Western National Parks Association, 2011.

———. *Great Smoky Mountains National Park: A Natural History Guide.* Boston: Houghton Mifflin Company, 1993.

———. *The Natural History Guide of the GSMNP.* New York: Houghton-Mifflin, 1993.

———. "The Salamander Capital of the World." *Smokies Life* 3, no. 2.

Hunt, Edward. "Building Roads through the Smokies." *Smoky Mountain Historical Society Newsletter* Xlll, no. 2 (Summer 1987).

Hunter, Chuck, et al. "Partners in Flight Bird Conservation Plan for the Southern Blue Ridge." Atlanta: USFWS, December 1999. www.partnersinflight.org/bcps/plan/pl_23_10.pdf

Hutson, Robert W., William F. Hutson, and Aaron J. Sharp. *Great Smoky Mountain Wildflowers,* 5th edition. Northbrook, IL: Windy Pines Press, 2006.

Jeffrey, Thomas E. *Thomas Lanier Clingman, Fireeater from the Carolina Mountains.* Athens: University of Georgia Press, 1998.

———. "'A Whole Torrent of Mean and Malevolent Abuse': Party Politics and the Clingman-Mitchell Controversy, Part 1." *North Carolina Historical Review* LXX, no. 3. Raleigh, NC: Division of Archives and History, July 1993.

———. "'A Whole Torrent of Mean and Malevolent Abuse': Party Politics and the Clingman-Mitchell Controversy, Part II." *North Carolina Historical Review* LXX, no. 4. Raleigh, NC: Division of Archives and History, October 1993.

Johnson, Kristine, Glenn Taylor, and Thomas Remaley. "Managing Hemlock Woolly Adelgid and Balsam Woolly Adelgid at Great Smoky Mountains

Bibliography

National Park." Presentation at Third Symposium on Hemlock Woolly Adelgid. www.na.fs.fed.us/fhp/hwa/pubs/proceedings/2005_proceedings/.

Jolley, Harley. *"'That Magnificent Army of Youth and Peace,' the Civilian Conservation Corps in NC, 1933–1942."* Raleigh: NC Office of Archives and History, 2007.

Justice, William S., and C. Ritchie Bell. *Wildflowers of NC.* Chapel Hill: University of North Carolina Press, 1968.

Keller, Becky. "Calcium Limitations to Southern Appalachian Songbirds." *Appalachian Highlands Science Journal,* January 2011.

Kelly, Chris. *Northern Flying Squirrel Habitat Management.* Annual Performance Report July 2009–June 2010. Wildlife Diversity Program, NCWC, Raleigh, NC.

Kemp, Steve. *Trees of the Smokies.* Gatlinburg, TN: GSMA, 2006.

Kemp, Steve, et al. *Hiking Trails of the Smokies,* 4th edition. Gatlinburg, TN: GSMA, 2009.

Kephart, Horace. *Our Southern Highlanders.* Knoxville: University of Tennessee Press, reprinted 1976.

King, Phillip B., and Arthur Stupka. "The Great Smoky Mountains—Their Geology and Natural History." *Scientific Monthly* 71, no. 1 (July 1950).

Kulp, Matt. Aquatics Specialists. Presentation: "Experience the Smokies: Behind-the-Scenes Tour," 2012.

"Land of the Sky." Promotional brochure, 1929. UNCA Special Collections, Asheville, NC.

Laufenberg, Jared. "Black Bear Ecology." Presentation: Southern Appalachian Naturalist's Certification Program. GSM Institute at Tremont, GSMNP. November 3, 2012.

———. "Black Bear 2006–2007 Den Season Update." www.fieldtripearth.org. January 12, 2012.

Laughlin, Jennifer. *Roan Mountain: A Passage of Time.* Winston-Salem, NC: John F. Blair, 1993.

Ledford, Jerry. Personal conversation. December 9, 2012.

Leitch, Alexander. *A Princeton Companion.* Princeton, NJ: Princeton University Press, 1978.

Letter from Dept. of Interior to Clingmans Dome Tower Project Supervisor Wilhelm, March 10, 1959. GSMNP Archives.

Letter from Middle Tennessee State University to GSMNP regarding Hubert Bebb credentials. GSMNP Archives, 1958.

Letter from Superintendent J.R. Eakin to Herbert Sass re: retaining "Clingmans Dome" as official name. GSMNP Archives: March 6, 1937.

Linzey, Donald W. *Mammals of GSMNP.* Blacksburg, VA: McDonald and Woodward Publishing Co.: 1995.

———. *A Natural History Guide to the GSMNP.* Knoxville: University of Tennessee Press, 2008.

Lix, Courtney. *Frequently Asked Questions about Smoky Mountain Bears.* Gatlinburg, TN: GSMA, 2010.

Loeb, Susan C., Frank H. Tainter, and Efren Cazares. "Habitat Associations of Hypogeous Fungi in the Southern Appalachians: Implications for the Endangered Northern Flying Squirrel *(Glaycomys sabrinus coloratus).*" *American Midland Naturalist* 144 (2000): 286–96.

Masterson, Linda. *Living with Bears.* Masonville, CO: PixyJack Press, 2006.

McManamay, Rachel, et al. "Assessing the Impacts of Balsam Woolly Adelgid *(Adelges piceae* Ratz.) and Anthropogenic Disturbance on the Stand Structure and Mortality of Fraser Fir *(Abies fraseri* (Pursh) Poir.) in the Black Mountains, NC." *Castenia* 76, no. 1 (March 2011): 1–19.

Meehan, Thomas. "Aconitum uncinatum: American Monkshood." *Meehan's Monthly, a Magazine of Horticulture, Botany, and Kindred Subjects* IV and V (1894).

Mellor, Lee. Personal interview. Buckhorn Inn, Gatlinburg, TN. January 2013.

Memorandum from Clingmans Dome Tower Project supervisor to Park superintendent regarding WC Norris Construction Co. April 10, 1939. GSMNP Archives:

Memorandum to NP Superintendent summarizing controversies expressed in *Knoxville News-Sentinel* regarding construction of Clingmans Dome Tower and "Modernistic Architecture and National Park Values." April 25, 1959. GSMNP Archives.

Milne, Lorus and Margery. *Because of a Flower.* New York: Atheneum, 1975.

Molloy, Johnny. *Day and Overnight Hikes, GSMNP.* Birmingham, AL: Menasha Ridge Press, 2008.

Mooney, James. *Myths of the Cherokee and Sacred Formulas of the Cherokee.* Nashville, TN: Charles and Randy Elder-Booksellers, Reproduced 1982.

Moore, Harry L. *A Roadside Guide to the Geology of the GSMNP.* Knoxville: University of Tennessee Press, 1988.

"NC Ecosystems Response to Climate Changes: DENR Assessment of Effects and Adaptation Measures." *Environmental reports, Appendix J,* August 27, 2010: Tennessee Valley Authority, NRP@tva.gov.

Newcombe, Lawrence. *Newcombe's Wildflower Guide.* Boston: Little, Brown, and Co., 1977.

BIBLIOGRAPHY

Noss, Reed F., Edward T. LaRoe III, and J. Michael Scott. *Endangered Ecosystems of the United States: A Preliminary Assessment of Loss and Degradation.* www.k-state.edu/withlab/consbiol/endangeredeco.pdf.

Ogburn, Charlton. *The Southern Appalachians: A Wilderness Quest.* New York: William Morrow & Co, 1975.

Owle, Raymond. "The Magic Lake." In *Living Stories of the Cherokee*, edited by Barbara R. Duncan. Chapel Hill: University of North Carolina Press, 1998.

"Pieces of the Past." (Railroad history below Clingmans Dome with Jerry Ledford). *Heartland Series* video. Knoxville: WBIR News, 2003.

Pierce, Daniel. *The Great Smokies from Habitat to National Park.* Knoxville: University of Tennessee Press, 2000.

"Pigeon Brings Word Back from Hills." *Asheville Times* XXXIII, no. 87. June 10, 1929.

Pivorun, Edward, et al. *Mammals of the Smokies.* Gatlinburg, TN: GSMA, 2009.

Price, Jackson E. Letter from associate director of GSMNP to Congressman David M. Hall regarding construction of Clingmans Dome Tower. GSMNP Archives, March 9, 1959.

Pyare, S., and W.S. Longland. "Mechanisms of Truffle Detection by Northern Flying Squirrels." *Canadian Journal of Zoology* 79 (2001): 1007–1015.

Pyle, Charlotte. "CCC Camps in the Great Smoky Mountains National Park." Unpublished manuscript at GSMNP Library, 1979.

Ragenovich, Iral R., and Russell G. Mitchell. "Forest Insect and Disease Leaflet 118: Balsam Woolly Adelgid." U.S. Department of Agriculture, USFS, revised May 2006.

Rankin, Duke. "Plant of the Week: Pirate Bush (*Buckleya distichophylla*)." USDA Forest Service, May 9, 2011.

"Red Crossbills: Tennessee's Watchable Wildlife." Web: //www.tnwatchablewildlife.org.

Renfro, Jim. "Air Quality of GSMNP" presentation at Clingmans Dome during the "Experience the Smokies; Behind-the-Scenes-Tour." 2012.

Renton, John. *The Nature of Earth: An Introduction to Geology.* (DVD). Chantilly, VA: The Teaching Co. 2006.

Robbins, Tom. (Retired ranger, GSMNP). Personal conversation. October 24, 2012.

Roth, Albert G. "Dutch." *The Roth Field Journal.* Knoxville: University of Tennessee Digital Libraries Initiatives, 1924–59.

Sachs, Susan. Workshop: "Science in the Park at Purchase Knob." GSMNP. July 2011.

Bibliography

Schmidt, Ronald G., and William S. Hooks. *Whistle Over the Mountain: Timber, Track, and Trails In the Tennessee Smokies.* Yellow Springs, OH: Graphicom Press, 1994.

Schwarzkopf, S. Kent. *A History of Mount Mitchell and the Black Mountains: Exploration, Development, and Preservation.* Raleigh, NC: North Carolina Division of Archives and History, 1985.

Sellars, Richard West. *Preserving Nature in the National Parks.* New Haven, CT: Yale Press, 1997.

Settlage, Katie. "A Thirty-five Year Study of Black Bears: Measurement and Data Collection in the Field." www.fieldtripearth.org. November 12, 2002.

Sibley, David Allen. *Sibley Guide to Birds.* New York: Alfred A. Knopf, 2000.

———. *Sibley Guide to Trees.* New York: Alfred A. Knopf, 2009.

Sidebottom, Jill. "Balsam Woolly Adelgid." NC Cooperative Extension Service. www.ces.ncsu.edu/fletcher/programs/xmas/ctnotes/ctn020.html.

———. "Why Fraser Fir? Chapter 2, History of the NC Christmas Tree..." NC Cooperative Extension Service. NCSU. www.ces.ncsu.edu/fletcher/programs/xmas/history/chapter2.html.

Silver, Timothy. *Mount Mitchell and the Black Mountains: An Environmental History of the Highest Peaks in Eastern America.* Chapel Hill: University of North Carolina Press, 2003.

Simmons, Morgan. "Retired Wildlife Professor Receives Prestigious Honor." http://m.knoxnews.com/news/2012. November 5, 2012.

———. "Tracking Tarantulas, Smokies Biologist Surveying Spruce-fir Moss Spider." *Knoxville News-Sentinel*, 2010.

Slapcinsky, John D. "Invertebrate of the Month: *Mesodon altivagus* (Pilsbry, 1900), "wandering Globe snail." Florida Museum of Natural History: Invertebrate Zoology. www.flmnh.ufl.edu/malacology/maltivagus.htm.

Small, John Kunkel. *Manual of Southeastern Flora. Vol. I–II.* Chapel Hill: University of North Carolina Press, 1933.

Smith, Arthur Wayne. "A 'Sky-Post' for the Smokies." *National Park Magazine* 33, no. 137 (February 1959).

Smith, Richard. *Wild Plants of America, a Select Guide for the Naturalist and Traveler.* New York: Wiley Nature Editions, 1989.

"Smokies Guide: Official Newspaper of GSMNP"; Special Report: "State of the Park." Fall 2011.

"Smokies Trails and Tales: Trails Forever-by the Numbers." www.FriendsOfTheSmokies.org.

Sondley, F.A. *A History of Buncombe County North Carolina.* Asheville, NC: The Advocate Printing Co., 1930.

Bibliography

Southworth, Scott. "Appalachian Blue Ridge Project: Mt. Le Conte Geological Study." USGS, June 2005.

Spira, Timothy P. *Wildflowers and Plant Communities of the Southern Appalachian Mountains and Piedmont.* Chapel Hill: University of North Carolina Press, 2011.

"Spruce-fir Moss Spider." You-Tube. Glenn Taylor and DLIA. GSMNP. www.youtube.com/watch?v=KvASW9LZesw.

"Spruce-fir Moss Spider (*Microhexura montivaga*)." Asheville, NC: USFWS, Dec. 2011.

Stewart, Kevin, and Mary-Russell Roberson. *Exploring the Geology of the Carolinas.* Chapel Hill: University of North Carolina Press, 2007.

Strutin, Michal. *History Hikes of the Smokies.* Gatlinburg, TN: GSMA, 2003.

Stupka, Arthur. "Birds of the Great Smokies: Spruce-Fir Avian Life Shows a Northern Character. *The Regional Review* IV, nos. 4 and 5 (April–May 1940).

———. *Notes on the Birds of GSMNP.* Knoxville: University of Tennessee Press, 1963.

———. "Smoky Mountains Cradle of Present-day Eastern Flora." *Asheville Citizen-Times*, January 2, 1938.

———. *Trees, Shrubs, and Woody Vines of GSMNP.* Knoxville: University of Tennessee Press, 1964.

———. *Wildflowers in Color.* New York: Harper and Row, 1965.

Sullivan, Janet. "Picea rubens." *Fire effects Information System (online).* USFS, Rocky Mountain Research Station, Fire Sciences Lab. http://www.fs.fed.us/dataabase/feis/ (2012, March).

Tager, Miles. *Grandfather Mountain: A Profile.* Boone, NC: Parkway Publishers (distributed by John F. Bair Publishing Co., Winston-Salem NC.), 1999.

Tate, Jane, and Michael Pelton. "Human-bear interactions in GSMNP." *Int. Conf. Bear Research and Management* 5 (1978): 312–21. www.bearbiology.com/fileadmin/tpl/Downloads/URSUS/Vol_5/Tate_Pelton_Vol_5.pdf.

Teale, Edwin Way. *North with the Spring.* New York: Dodd, Mead, and Co., 1957.

Tekiela, Stan. *Birds of the Carolinas Field Guide and Audio CD.* Cambridge, MN: Adventure Public, Inc., 2004.

Thompson, Roger B. "Describes Observation Tower in Park as Actually the Continuation of a Trail." *Knoxville News-Sentinel*, February 18, 1959.

Thornborough, Laura. *The Great Smoky Mountains.* 9th edition. Knoxville: University of Tennessee Press, 1967.

Bibliography

Tilley, Stephen, and James E. Huheey. *Reptiles and Amphibians of the Smokies.* Gatlinburg, TN: GSMA, 2001.

"Times' Explorers Tell Experiences in Great Smokies." *Asheville Times*, July 5, 1929.

Trotter, Thomas. Trotter and Associates, Architect. Personal communication. January 2013.

Trotter, William R. *Bushwhackers, Civil War in NC, the Mountains.* Winston-Salem, NC: John F. Blair Publ., 1988.

U.S. Dept. of Agriculture: USFS. *The Beginnings of the National Forests in the South: Protection of Watersheds.* Washington, D.C.: June 4, 2003. www.forestinhistory.org/ASPNET/policy/WeeksAct/ProtectionofWatersheds_Williams.pdf.

———. "High level problem for Songbirds." *Compass.* Washington: Southern Research Station. February 2008.

———. "Management Guide for Balsam Woolly Adelgid." Washington, D.C.: March 2010. www.fs.usda.gov/Internet/FSE_DOCUMENTS/stelprdb5187218.pdf.

———. Southeast Region. "Stressors of Spruce-fir Forests: Balsam Woolly Adelgid." *The Health of Forests.* July 5, 2012. www.fs.fed.us/r8/foresthealth/host/bwa.htm.

U.S. Department of Energy. "Clean Coal Technology." Fossil Energy Office of Communications. www.fossilenergy.gov/programs/powersystems/cleancoal.

U.S. Department of Interior, GSMNP. "Air Quality." Gatlinburg, TN: GSMA, March 2006.

———. "Air Quality Update." NPS Briefing Statement, April 26, 2010.

———. "Black Bears." www.nps.gov/grsm/.

———. "Calcium Limitations in Southern Appalachian Songbirds." Gatlinburg, TN: GSMA, January 2011.

———. "NPS Profile: Air Above and Beyond the Smokies." Gatlinburg, TN: GSMA, July 22, 2010.

———. "State of the Park." *Smokies Guide.* Gatlinburg, TN: GSMA, February 2011.

———. "Water Quality." Gatlinburg, TN: GSMA, May 2011.

U.S. Department of Interior, NPS. Air Resources Division. "Air Quality in the National Parks." September 2002. www.nature.nps.gov/air/.

U.S. Energy Information Administration. "Coal and the Environment." October 20, 2011. www.eia.gov/coal/.

U.S. EPA. "Effects of Acid Rain: Surface Waters and Aquatic Animals." December 1, 2008. www.epa.gov/acidrain/effects/surface_water.html.

Bibliography

———. *The Plain English Guide to the Clean Air Act.* April 2007. www.epa.gov/air/peg/pdfs/ped.pdf.

USGS. "Geology of GSMNP, TN and NC." *Geological Survey Bulletin.* www.cr.nps.gov/history/online_books/geology/publications/pp/587/index.html.

Van Manen, Frank. "Long-term Black Bear Research Program in GSMNP." www.fieldtripearth.org.

"Vegetation: Summer 2010." GSMNP: Resource Round-up, no 8. http://www.nps.gov/grsm/naturescience/dff8-vegetation.htm.

Waddell, Maude. "South Gives Nation its Most Beautiful Playground: Carolina and Tennessee Contribute Great Smokies to National Park System." *Charlotte Observer,* January 18, 1931.

Wadley, Jeff, and Dwight McCarter. *Mayday! Mayday! Aircraft Crashes of the GSMNP, 1920–2000.* Knoxville: University of Tennessee Press, 2002.

Wagner, Frederic, et al. *Wildlife Policies in the National Parks.* Washington, D.C.: Island Press, 1995.

"WC Norris Co. Will Construct Unique Tower atop Clingmans Dome." *Waynesville Mtn. News,* December 8, 1958.

Weals, Vic. *Last Train to Elkmont.* Kodak, TN: Olden Press, 1993.

Weidensaul, Scott. *Mountains of the Heart: A Natural History of the Appalachians.* Golden, CO: Fulcrum Publishing Co., 2004, reissue of 1994 ed.

Weigl, Peter D. "The Northern Flying Squirrel (*Glaucomys sabrinus*): A Conservation Challenge." *Journal of Mammology* 88, no. 4 (2007): 897–907.

Whaley, Diana. "Hubert Bebb: Architect's works reflect his love of Smoky Mountains." *Gatlinburg Press* (now *Mountain Press*), August 29, 1983.

White, Peter, Tom Condon, Janet Rock, Carol Ann McCormick, Pat Beaty, and Keith Langdon. *Wildflowers of the Smokies.* Gatlinburg, TN: GSMA, 1996.

Williams, Dan D. *The Forests of GSMNP.* Athens, GA: Possum Publishing, 2011.

Williams, Don. "Dutch Roth, Legacy of a Photographer." *Smokies Life* 4, no. 1. Gatlinburg: GSMA.

Wise, Kenneth. *Hiking Trails of the Great Smoky Mountains, a Comprehensive Guide.* Knoxville: University of Tennessee Press, 1996.

Wise, Kenneth, and Ron Peterson. *A Natural History of Mt Le Conte.* Knoxville: University of Tennessee Press, 1998.

"Word Brought from Hills by Homing Pigeon." *Asheville Times* XXXIII, no. 88. June 11, 1929.

Zahner, Robert. *The Mountain at the End of the Trail: A History of Whiteside Mountain.* Highlands, NC: self-published, 1994.

INDEX

A

acid rain 78, 130, 134, 135
Agassiz, Louis 26
air quality monitoring station 131, 156
Anakeesta Formation 127
Andrews Bald 47, 58, 98, 100, 110, 150, 151, 161
Appalachian Trail 30, 38, 81, 98, 101, 113, 119, 137, 140, 143, 162, 165, 166
automated cloud collector 131
Avery, Myron 31

B

ballhooting 151
Balsam Mountain 90, 159
Balsam Mountain Road 87
balsam woolly adelgid 71, 73, 83, 85, 144, 165
   Clingmans Dome impact 87
   Fraser fir response 86
   life cycle 88, 89
   monitoring 90
   scientific study/future 92
Bartram, William 162, 164
bats
   little brown bat 80
Bebb, Hubert 60
birds
   American robin 82, 109
   Blackburnian warblers 75, 141
   black-capped chickadee 76
   black-throated blue warbler 78
   black-throated green warbler 75, 141
   blue-headed vireo 78
   brown creeper 76, 141
   Canada warbler 82
   cedar waxwing 81, 109
   chestnut-sided warbler 82
   dark-eyed junco 80, 135
   eastern towhee 82

Index

golden-crowned kinglet 76
gray catbird 82
hairy woodpecker 75
northern raven 82
northern saw-whet owl 76
olive-sided flycatcher 81
pine siskin 81
red-breasted nuthatch 76
red crossbill 81
veery 80, 141
white pelicans 81
winter wren 46, 76, 141
Black Mountains 25, 26, 86
Blanket Mountain 156
Bluff Mountain 157
Bratton, Susan 52
Broome, Harvey 143
Buckley, Samuel 24, 30, 103, 138, 157, 158, 165

C

Cades Cove 37, 113, 119, 131, 150, 151, 165, 166
Campbell, Carlos 52
Camp Kephart 55
Cataloochee 87, 150, 159
Champion Fibre 46
Cheoah Bald 164
Cherohala Skyway 75
Cherokee Indians 18, 51, 138, 145, 159, 160, 161, 162, 164, 165
Cherokee, North Carolina 24, 55, 160
Chimney Tops 47, 48, 127, 146, 155, 157
Civilian Conservation Corps (CCC) 30, 54, 57, 138, 141, 145, 151, 158
Civil War 31, 87, 137, 145, 160
Clean Coal Technology 133
Clingman, Thomas Lanier 21, 22, 24, 25, 26, 29, 32, 35, 51, 70, 103, 138, 158, 159, 165
Cold Mountain 25, 160
Collins, Robert 26, 141, 157
concretions 126
copper mine 145
Cove Mountain 131, 156
Coyle, Dr. Fredrick 71

D

Devil's Courthouse Ridge 40, 141
Dickerman, Ernie 143
Donati's comet 22
Double Springs Gap 144

E

Eakin, Superintendent J.R. 81, 148
Elkmont 37, 38, 119, 131, 144, 148, 156, 157
Environmental Protection Agency 130, 133, 135

F

ferns
  intermediate wood 79
  mountain wood fern 79
  southern lady fern 79
Fink, Paul 35, 52
Fontana Dam 162, 164
Fontana Lake 41, 135, 139, 140, 150, 152, 162, 164
Fontana Village 41, 162
Fork Ridge Trail 146
Forney Creek 40, 41, 43, 45, 47, 57, 103, 150, 152, 164
Forney Ridge 40, 45, 47, 100, 103, 108, 141, 150, 151, 152, 161
Fry Mountain 161

Index

G

Gatlinburg 37, 127, 157, 165
glacier 69, 123
Goshen Prong 38, 103, 119, 144
Grandfather Mountain 70, 71, 72
grass, Smoky Mountain manna 151
Gregory Bald 137, 165
Gregory, Russell 165
Grotto Falls 157
ground-level ozone 130, 131
Guyot, Arnold 3, 21, 24, 26, 32, 51, 150, 157, 158, 159, 165, 174
Guyot's map 30

H

Harp, Dr. Joel 72
Hay, Dr. Robert 87
High Rocks 164

I

Indian Gap 52, 58, 81, 98, 127, 141, 143, 145, 146, 160
insecticidal soap 87
intrusion 126

J

Johnson, Kristine 87, 90, 91
Junaluska, Chief 163
Juvabione 92

K

Kulp, Matt 130, 135

L

Le Conte, John 25, 157
lichens
  old man's beard 75

Little River 37, 38, 134
Little River Lumber Company 37, 38, 41
Little River Road 146
Little Tennessee River 135, 162
log loader 41
London's "Killer Smog" 133
Love, Colonel Robert H. 26
Love, Samuel 24

M

mammals
  bobcat 80, 117
  Carolina northern flying squirrel 74, 163
  coyote 79
  deer mouse 76
  European wild boar 137, 141
  long-tailed shrew 79
  long-tailed weasel 79
  masked shrew 79
  raccoon 79
  red fox 79
  red squirrel 74, 141
  rock vole 76
  Smoky shrew 79
  southern flying squirrel 74
  southern red-backed vole 76
  striped skunk 79
  Virginia opossum 79
Mission 66 60
Mitchell, Elisha 22, 159
Mountains-to-Sea Trail (MST) 148
Mount Buckley 29, 72, 91, 99, 103, 119, 140, 144, 151, 165, 166
Mount Collins 29, 35, 71, 81, 88, 141, 146, 157
Mount Craig 29, 159
Mount Guyot 47, 48, 87, 88, 91, 158

INDEX

Mount Kephart 29, 157
Mount Le Conte 71, 72, 90, 127, 157
Mount Love 29, 72, 91, 143
Mount Mingus 24
Mount Mitchell 22, 25, 26, 28, 29, 70, 71, 72, 74, 86, 159
Mount Pisgah 22, 25, 29, 32, 159, 160
Mount Rogers 70, 86, 92
Mount Sterling 86, 88, 90, 164

N

Nantahala Gorge 162, 164
Nantahala Mountains 56, 162, 164
Nantahala National Forest 161, 164
Nantahala Ranger District 162
Nantahala slate 164
Newfound Gap 24, 55, 58, 98, 127, 141, 143, 145, 148, 157, 158
Newfound Gap Road 55, 58, 119, 127, 146, 150, 151, 158, 160
Newton Bald 159
nitrogen oxide 130, 133, 134

O

Oconaluftee Fault 127
Oconaluftee River 24, 127, 160

P

Pangea 122
particulate matter 134
Pelton, Dr. Michael 115
Purchase Knob 93, 131, 134, 159
pyrite 127

Q

Qualla Boundary 160

R

railroad 138, 144, 151, 152
Railroad 31, 32, 37, 38, 40
Rainbow Falls 125, 157
Ramsey Cascades 30, 159
Renfro, Jim 130, 133, 134, 136
rime ice 143
Ritter Lumber Company 41, 164
Road Prong 127, 145
Roan Mountain 70, 72, 74, 172
Roaring Fork 157
Rock Slab Falls 152
Roosevelt, President Franklin D. 54, 158
Roosevelt, Theodore 35
Rugel, Ferdinand 24, 103

S

salamanders
  Cheoah salamander 164
  imitator salamanders 79
  pygmy salamander 79
Save the Smokies Hike 138, 144
shrubs, bushes and brambles 137
  Catawba rhododendron 110, 151
  dog hobble 95
  flame azalea 110, 150, 151, 161, 165
  highbush blueberry 95
  red elderberry 96
  thornless blackberry 82, 97
Shuckstack Mountain 164
Silers Bald 40, 81, 108, 143, 145, 164, 166
Sky-Post 65
Skyway Drive 143
Smokemont 47, 58, 159
Smoky Dome 3, 21, 22, 25, 28, 158
Smoky Mountain Hiking Club 52

Index

snails
  Mesodon altivagus 78
  Vitrinizonites latissumus 79
snakes
  black rat snake 79
  timber rattlesnake 79
Snowbird Mountains 163, 164
spruce-fir moss spider 71, 144, 165
Standing Indian Mountain 161
Stiver, Bill 113
Stupka, Arthur 81
Sugarland Mountain 127, 146, 157
sulfur 104, 134

T

Taylor, Glenn 72
Tennessee River 134
Thomas Divide 159
Thomas Ridge 160
Thomas, William 51, 160
Thornborough, Laura 30
Three Forks 38, 144
Thunderhead Mountain 37, 125, 165
Thunderhead sandstone 125, 126, 164, 165
Trail of Tears 51, 163
trees
  balsam fir 70, 85
  European silver fir 85
  Fraser fir 45, 61, 70, 74, 76, 78, 82, 86, 90, 92, 97, 111, 127, 134, 139, 144, 165
  mountain ash 78, 81, 82, 97, 112
  mountain maple 82
  pin cherry 81, 82, 97
  red spruce 45, 70, 134
  yellow birch 76, 82, 97, 137, 150
Tremont 37, 40, 134

Tricorner Knob 159
Tsali 148
Tuckasegee River 41, 135, 162

U

U.S. Clean Air Act 133

V

volatile orgainc compounds (VOC) 130

W

watershed 135, 150, 157, 162
Waynesville 22, 25, 26, 28, 64
W. C. Norris Construction Company 64
Weigl, Dr. Peter 75
Welch Ridge 150, 164
wildflowers
  bluebead or Clinton's lily 98, 143
  Blue Ridge St. John's wort 24
  Canada mayflower 98
  Clingmans hedge-nettle 100
  crimson bee-balm 100
  cutleaf coneflower 103, 134
  erect trillium 98
  filmy angelica 107
  large purple-fringed orchid 100
  Michaux's saxifrage 107
  mountain gentian 108
  mountain St. John's wort 107
  mountain wood-sorrel 99
  nodding ladies' tresses 100
  painted trillium 97
  pink turtlehead 109, 143
  purple-flowering raspberry 82, 109
  rosy twisted stalk 98
  Rugel's Indian plantain 24, 101, 141, 144, 165

Index

skunk goldenrod 104, 107
small purple-fringed orchid 100
stiff gentian 108
Turk's cap lily 99
white snakeroot 104
whorled wood aster 104
wild monkshood 108
yellow trout lily 99

ABOUT THE AUTHOR

A master's of science degree from East Tennessee State University prepared Marci for a career as a nurse practitioner in the fields of cardiology, family practice and overseas medical missionary service. Weekends found her piloting a private airplane or climbing a mountain somewhere. Now retired, and thousands of hiking-miles later, Marci volunteers for Great Smoky Mountains National Park in resource development at Clingmans Dome. Thirty years of independent nature study became more structured in an interpretative natural science program at the North Carolina Arboretum, earning her certification as a Blue Ridge Naturalist. Currently, she's enrolled in the Southern Appalachian Naturalist's course at Tremont in the Smokies. As a volunteer for a bear rescue center, she is a school educator on black bears. A 2012 finalist in the Grateful Steps Publishing Company's writing contest, her short story, "Instincts," was e-published in a collection of winners.

Visit us at
www.historypress.net

This title is also available as an e-book

www.ingramcontent.com/pod-product-compliance
Lightning Source LLC
Chambersburg PA
CBHW070344100426
42812CB00005B/1428